Van Nostrand's
Plain English
Handbook

Stanley W. Lindberg
University of Georgia

J. Martyn Walsh
Anna Kathleen Walsh

D. VAN NOSTRAND COMPANY
New York   Cincinnati   Toronto   London   Melbourne

D. Van Nostrand Company Regional Offices:
New York   Cincinnati

D. Van Nostrand Company International Offices:
London   Toronto   Melbourne

Copyright © 1980 by Litton Educational Publishing, Inc.

Library of Congress Catalog Card Number: 79-55943
ISBN: 0-442-26355-4

Published by D. Van Nostrand Company
135 West 50th Street, New York, N. Y. 10020

10 9 8 7 6 5 4 3 2 1

Preface

This book is intended to provide a complete but concise introduction to the basic conventions of American English. It is not organized as a comprehensive survey of rhetorical tactics; nor does it attempt to discuss linguistical theory, semiotics, or structural and transformational grammar. We have focused instead on the fundamentals, aiming to present the accepted practices of standard usage in a manner that can serve as both a classroom text and a practical lifetime guide for the writer.

In many important ways, *Van Nostrand's Plain English Handbook* continues the tradition of the highly respected *Plain English Handbook,* first published in 1939 by J. Martyn Walsh and Anna Kathleen Walsh (and currently in its seventh revised edition). The new *Van Nostrand's Plain English Handbook* represents a concerted effort to provide college students and adults with a thorough introduction to the basics within a book of manageable size and scope. New features include chapters on "From Paragraph to Essay," "The Research Paper," and "Using the Library." An integral part of this text is the inclusion of practical exercises, interspersed throughout the text to illustrate immediately the conventions being presented.

To the extent possible, each chapter of this book is essentially self-contained, allowing users to consult or study it in sequences other than its present arrangement. The sections are numbered consecutively to make effective cross-referencing possible. Numbers within parentheses refer to other sections within the book.

Contents

Sentence Completeness

Effective sentences result from applying many functional elements: good logic, good syntax and grammar, good organization of ideas, careful variation to avoid monotony, and proper emphasis in setting forth important thoughts and images. To a large extent, effectiveness is dependent upon the proper use of modifiers. It is the sentence modifiers that qualify and particularize, giving the sentence the clarity and precision that is the purpose of good writing.

THE SENTENCE AND ITS PARTS

1   A **sentence** is a word or a group of words that expresses and conveys a complete thought from a speaker or writer to a listener or reader. When written, it begins with a capital letter and closes with a terminal mark of punctuation.

The book is on the table.

2   A sentence must have a **subject** and a **predicate**, either expressed or implied (understood), and—as will be shown—it may have an object complement or other complements, modifiers, connectives, and independent elements.

3   The **subject** is that about which something is said:

Flowers bloom.   *Shakespeare* wrote many great plays.
Squirrels climb trees.   *Denver* is in Colorado.

4   The **predicate** is that which is said about the subject:

Flowers *bloom.*   Shakespeare *wrote many great plays.*
Squirrels *climb trees.*   Denver *is in Colorado.*

DIAGRAM—Sentence with *simple subject* (13) and *simple predicate* (15):

Fish swim.

5   A sentence must have a subject and a predicate in order to be grammatically complete, but in an **elliptical sentence** (a sentence or clause from which a word or words are properly omitted) either the subject or the predicate or both may not be expressed:

Subject omitted: (*You*) Read this story.
Predicate omitted: Who spoke? John (*spoke*).
Subject and predicate verb omitted: What did I bring? (*I brought*) Books.

6   The receiver of the action denoted by the simple predicate (15) is the **direct object** (sometimes called the **object complement**):

The carpenter built a *house.*
The girls picked *corn.*

DIAGRAM—Sentence with *direct object* of a verb:

Farmers grow *wheat.*

The direct object may be **compound** (17):

We saw *rocks* and *trees.*

DIAGRAM—Sentence with *compound direct object of verb:*

Dad planted *shrubs* and *flowers.*

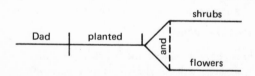

7   A **modifier** is a word or a group of words that qualifies and characterizes the meaning of another word:

She ran *quickly.* (*Quickly* modifies *ran.*)

The tall blond man laughed. (*The, tall,* and *blond* modify *man.*)

The boy *at the desk* is Fred. (*At the desk* modifies *boy.*)

The girl *whom you saw* is Jane. (*Whom you saw* modifies *girl.*)

DIAGRAM—Sentence with *modifiers* of subject and predicate:

The concerned young woman spoke *frankly.*

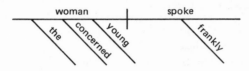

8   A group of related words not having a subject and a predicate is called a **phrase:**

The book *on the desk* is a grammar.

9   A group of related words having a subject and a predicate and used as a part of a sentence is called a **clause:**

Mary is the girl *who swam.* (Subject is *who;* predicate is *swam.*)

10   Although a sentence or a clause must have a subject and a predicate, either can be correct with only one word expressed:

Go. **(sentence)**

The coach said, "Go." **(clause)**

In both the sentence and the clause above, the omitted subject *you* is clearly understood.

11   **Connectives** (sometimes called **connectors**) serve to join the sentence parts:

He came *with* me. **(preposition, 44)**

Girls *and* boys play tennis. **(conjunction, 45)**

12   **Independent elements** are expressions that have no grammatical connection with the sentence in which they are found. They are of several kinds:

    a. **Interjection:** *Hurrah*! we won.

    b. **Direct address:** *Ruth,* I want you to help me.

    c. **Exclamation:** *Poor dog*! It needs our help.

    d. **Parenthetical limiting expression:** He went, *I am sure,* to please us.

    e. **Responsive:** *No,* he has not come.

    f. **Nominative absolute:** *The work being done,* we went home.

    Most independent elements are set off from the rest of the sentence by commas (500), whereas the interjection and the exclamation are set apart by an exclamation mark (531).

13   The **simple subject** is the subject taken without any modifier (7):

A noisy *crowd* gathered immediately.

The simple subject may consist of more than one word (**compound noun**, 60):

Betty Ruth Mills is a lawyer.
The *flour mill* burned down.

14   The **complete subject** is the simple subject with all its modifiers:

The first game began early.
The girl at the pool is Evelyn.

15   The **simple predicate** is the predicate taken without any modifier or complement. The simple predicate may consist of more than one word, for it may
include a main verb and its helpers (a **verb phrase**, 41):

The boy *has waited* patiently.
The book *should have been returned* to the library.

16   The **complete predicate** is the predicate with all its complements and modifiers:

The girl *has tried patiently.*
The visitor *has tried repeatedly.*

17   A **compound subject** is one made up of two or more simple subjects:

Flowers and *trees* are beautiful.

18   A **compound predicate** consists of two or more simple predicates:

Healthy children *work* and *play.*

19   Both the subject and predicate may be compound:

Girls and *boys study* and *play.*

DIAGRAM—Sentence with *compound subject* and *compound predicate:*

Boys and *girls play* and *sing.*

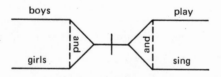

Exercise 1.1   Recognizing Subjects and Predicates.
Copy the following sentences on a separate sheet. Draw <u>one</u> line under the
simple subject. Draw <u>two</u> lines under the simple predicate.

EXAMPLE: <u>Can</u> <u>you</u> <u>recognize</u> subjects and predicates?

a.   Nearly every class member has paid his dues.
b.   That house on the corner is owned by my uncle.
c.   Was your answer to the problem correct?
d.   After lunch who will go with me?
e.   The person in blue is very tall and thin.
f.   He and I made our plans for the summer.

g. Several of the girls read books and listen to the radio at the same time.
h. Tell me the truth about your assignment.
i. Suzanne and Paul came to the meeting and spoke to us.
j. Jim and I will call the members and will arrange for transportation.

Exercise 1.2   Recognizing Essential Parts of the Sentence.
Copy the following sentences on a separate sheet. Draw one line under the complete subject and two lines under the complete predicate of each sentence. Then draw a box around the verb and (if there is one) circle the direct object.

EXAMPLE: Amelia Earhart |flew| her (plane) across the Atlantic by herself in 1932.

a. The airplane is the most amazing invention of the modern world.
b. Leonardo da Vinci drew the earliest known design for a helicopter about 1500.
c. Sir George Cayley frequently is called "the father of the airplane."
d. Otto Lilienthal's gliding research in 1895 led to the invention of the airplane.
e. The first successful fliers were the Wright brothers.
f. The first planes were largely built of canvas, bamboo, and steel wire.
g. During the early 1900's, daring pilots broke aviation records almost every week.
h. Baronne Raymonde de Laroche of France became the first licensed woman pilot in 1910.
i. The first airplane race in the United States was held in 1910.
j.   Charles Lindbergh made the first nonstop transatlantic solo flight in 1927.
k. In 1957 three jet bombers flew around the world in 45 hours.
l. Aviation has created new growth patterns for many cities of the world.
m. In some areas of the world rice is now sown from airplanes.
n. Airplanes are also used for crop dusting as well as for air freight.
o. Many private persons now pilot their own airplanes.

CLASSIFICATION OF SENTENCES

20 Sentences are classified according to their structure or form, as **simple, compound**, and **complex**. (A less common type, the **compound-complex**, is described in section 416.)

21 **A simple sentence** has only one independent clause (397) and no dependent clause (398):

Our team won the game.

Both the subject and predicate of a simple sentence may be compound (19):

Mark and Ruth played and sang at the party. (A simple sentence may have any number of phrases—*at the party* is a phrase—but it cannot contain a dependent clause.)

22   A **compound sentence** is equivalent to two or more simple sentences (called **independent clauses** when used in a single sentence) connected by **coordinating conjunctions** (367) or by punctuation:

> Joe studies hard and he enjoys school.
> Joe studies hard; he enjoys school.
> Joe studies hard. He enjoys school.

Notice the three ways of writing these words. The last way is not a compound sentence; it is two simple sentences.

23   A **complex sentence** is one that contains but *one* independent clause (397) and one or more dependent clauses (398):

> I was not at home when he came. (The clause *when he came* is dependent.)

♦ Although the definition for the complex sentence given above is the conventional one, there is another type of complex sentence in which the independent clause is not at once evident. In this type a noun clause (400–407) may be an essential element of the independent clause:

> *That she is intelligent* is obvious. (**subject**)
> The truth *is that he forgot.* (**predicate nominative**)
> She said *that she would accept the offer.* (**object**)

24   As to function, sentences are divided into four classes: **declarative, imperative, interrogative**, and **exclamatory**.

25   A **declarative sentence** makes a statement or asserts a fact:

> Our glee club sings well.

26   The **imperative sentence** expresses a command, request, or entreaty:

> Do not walk on the grass. (The subject of an imperative sentence is *you*; it is usually omitted.)

27   The **interrogative sentence** asks a question:

> Where shall we go?   Whom will we meet?   What will we do?

28   The **exclamatory sentence** expresses surprise or a strong emotion:

> What are they up to now!   How beautiful the sunset is!

A declarative, an interrogative, or an imperative sentence may also become exclamatory when expressed excitedly; therefore, not all grammarians list the exclamatory sentence as a separate class.

29   The **natural** or **normal order** of the sentence is for the subject to precede the predicate:

> George went to school.

30   When the complete predicate or some part of it precedes the subject, the sentence is in **inverted order**. In an interrogative sentence (27) and in a sentence beginning with the expletive (239) *there* or the adverbs *here* or *there*, the predicate or a part of it usually precedes the subject:

> Have you *received* the book?
> There *are* three books on the desk.
> *There* your book *will be found.*
> Here *comes* Rose.

31   **END PUNCTUATION**   Correct punctuation at the end of a sentence is very important. The declarative sentence (25) ends with a period. The imperative sentence (26) ends with a period. The interrogative sentence (27) closes with a question mark. The exclamatory sentence (28) usually ends with an exclamation mark:

> The trees are most colorful in autumn. **(declarative)**
> Come to see me next winter. **(imperative)**
> Do you like English? **(interrogative)**
> How quiet these forests are! **(exclamatory)**

32   **CAPITALIZATION**   Every English sentence (except one in parentheses within another sentence) begins with a capital letter.

Exercise 1.3   Recognizing Sentences.
Classify each of the following sentences as declarative, interrogative, imperative, or exclamatory. Put in the proper end punctuation.

EXAMPLE: *Inter.* How can you improve your personality?
                                                            ∧

a. Be tactful and agreeable to all
b. Are you loyal to your friends
c. We should never find fault with other people
d. How unselfish she is
e. Do you make friends easily
f. We all like agreeable people
g. Try to improve your personality
h. What a pleasing manner she has
i.   Try to be considerate of older people
j. How well-liked thoughtful people always are

WRITING GOOD SENTENCES

33   **Do not omit the subject from a declarative sentence:**

> **Incorrect:** Saw you at the show last night.
> **Correct:** I saw you at the show last night.
> (Subjects are properly omitted from imperative sentences [26].)

34   **Do not write a fragment of a sentence as if it were complete:**

> **Incorrect:** He studied hard. Hoping to learn it all. (The words *hoping to*

learn it all form a phrase which modifies *he*.)

Correct: He studied hard, hoping to learn it all.

Incorrect: Anne had a good time. While she was in the East last summer. (The words *while she was in the East last summer* form a dependent clause used as an adverbial modifier.)

Correct: Anne had a good time while she was in the East last summer.

35 **Do not write two or more sentences together as one, without punctuation:**

Incorrect: We started early we were eager for the trip.
Correct: We started early. We were eager for the trip.
Correct: We started early; we were eager for the trip.

36 **Learn to distinguish a sentence from a fragment and from a group of more than one sentence.** An ability to distinguish between a sentence and a group of words which is more or less than a sentence is called **sentence sense.**

While we waited for the train. (This group of words, which resembles a dependent clause, is not a sentence; it is a fragment.)

Men and women running. (Because these words do not have a predicate they do not form a sentence.)

They are running. (This group of words is a sentence. It expresses a complete thought and has both a subject and a predicate.)

Ask your teacher to help you. (This is an imperative sentence. The subject *you* is understood.)

Janice plays basketball she is captain of the team. (Two sentences are incorrectly written as one. This can be corrected in three ways:

1. Janice plays basketball. She is captain of the team.
2. Janice plays basketball; she is captain of the team.
3. Janice plays basketball, and she is captain of the team.)

That was a good game our boys played well were you there? (Three sentences are incorrectly joined as one. This can be corrected: That was a good game. Our boys played well. Were you there?)

37 **Do not splice sentences or independent clauses together with a comma:**

Incorrect: My brother studies French, he hopes to be a translator. (Two sentences are incorrectly written as one.)
Correct: My brother studies French. He hopes to be a translator.

♦ Independent clauses *may* be connected with the semicolon (if they are closely related in content) or with *a comma and a conjunction:*

My brother studies French; he hopes to be a translator.
My brother studies French, and he hopes to be a translator.

Exercise 1.4   Sentence Sense.

Identify each of the following groups of words as a fragment, a complete sentence, or a run-on (more than one complete sentence).

EXAMPLE: *Run-on* Flags flutter from the stadium a runner carries a torch into the arena.

a. Every four years, amateur athletes from many nations compete in the Olympic Games.

b. The purpose of the Olympic Games to let the great amateur athletes compete.

c. The Summer Olympics run for about two weeks the Winter Olympics last ten days.

d. Relying on individual citizens to pay their Olympic expenses.

e. No other sport spectacle has a background so historic, dramatic, or thrilling.

f. Behind their flags the athletes march into the stadium they stand at attention.

g. A runner carries a blazing torch to announce the opening of the Olympic Games.

h. In the bob-sledding events, two- or four-member teams.

i. Nations do not actually compete against each other no nation officially wins.

j. In the ancient Olympics, sacrifices of grain, wine, and lambs.

k. The early games included competition in art forms as well as in athletics.

l. Criers announcing the winners' names throughout the land.

m. Women were excluded from the ancient Games as competitors and spectators.

n. If practiced in accordance with the ancient Greek ideals.

o. The exact date of the first games is unknown the first recorded race was in 776 B.C.

The Parts of Speech

A DEFINITION, formal and exact, must include all that belongs to the object defined and exclude all that does not; an EXPLANATION, general, may simply throw light upon some point of special difficulty; a DESCRIPTION, pictorial, may include only some general features. In all good writing these three concepts must always be distinguished so that the reader may readily understand the viewpoint of the writer.

DEFINITIONS

38   All words may be classified into eight groups called **parts of speech**. The group to which a word belongs is determined by its use in the sentence; therefore, the same word may be any one of several parts of speech, depending upon its use in a given sentence. The eight parts of speech are **noun, pronoun, verb, adjective, adverb, preposition, conjunction,** and **interjection**.

39   A **noun** is the name of a person, place, thing, idea, or quality.

Robert Frost wrote *poems.*   *Ann* lives in *Boston.*
Work brings *satisfaction.*   *People* like *admiration.*

40   A **pronoun** is a word used to take the place of a noun. Through its use, one may avoid repeating name words:

Mary has lost *her* book.   The box has lost *its* handle.
Ruth saw the boys and talked with *them.*

41 A **verb** is a word used to express action, being, or state of being:

José *painted* a picture.   The law still *exists*.
That woman *is* a banker.

A verb may be composed of several words, called a **verb phrase**:

This book *should have been sent* to the storeroom.

42 An **adjective** is used to modify a noun or a pronoun. An adjective may be a single word, a phrase, or a clause:

We saw *beautiful* valleys and *rugged* mountains. **(single words)**
The rug *on the floor* is blue. **(adjective phrase)**
The man *who spoke* is a teacher. **(adjective clause)**

43 An **adverb** is used to modify a verb, an adjective, or another adverb. It may be a single word, a phrase, or a clause:

He sang *beautifully*. **(single word)**
The stranger came *into the room*. **(adverbial phrase)**
Robert left *when I came*. **(adverbial clause)**

In some cases adverbs may modify other parts of speech (316).

44 A **preposition** shows the relation between its object and some other word in the sentence:

We walked through the woods. (*Through* shows the nature of the relation between *woods,* its object, and *walked,* the verb.)

45 A **conjunction** connects words or groups of words:

Bob *and* Linda are here.   She came *but* she did not stay.

46 An **interjection** expresses strong feeling: *Ouch! Oh!*

The interjection has no grammatical relation to the rest of the sentence.

47 A **substantive** is any word or group of words that is used as a noun (39) or as a noun equivalent (61).

48 **Inflection** is any change in the spelling or the form of a word to indicate a change in its meaning: *book–books, I–me, has–have.*

I *have* the *book* here.   He *has* the *books* for *me*.

49 The inflection of nouns and pronouns is called **declension** (144, 159): *man–men, he–him.*

He is a friendly *man*.   The *men* are with *him*.

50 The inflection of adjectives and adverbs is called **comparison** (295-327): *big–bigger–biggest, fast–faster–fastest.*

The *big* boy ran *fast,* and the *bigger* boy ran *faster,* but the *biggest* boy ran *fastest* of all.

51   The correct arrangement of the inflection of verbs is called **conjugation** (see 205).

52   The use and recorded meaning of a word in a given sentence determines what part of speech it is; therefore, while a word may be one part of speech in a particular sentence, it may be used as a different part of speech in another sentence:

> You must not *rock* the boat. (**verb,** 41)
> We saw a *rock* fence. (**adjective,** 42)
> That *rock* is beautiful. (**noun,** 39)
> The word *but* may be almost any part of speech. (**noun,** 39)
> We walked *but* a short distance. (**adverb,** 43)
> All came *but* Ann. (**preposition,** 44)
> We waited for him, *but* he did not come. (**conjunction,** 45)
> They made five yards on the first *down.* (**noun,** 39)
> Karen made a *down* payment on the car. (**adjective,** 42)
> We walked *down* the hill. (**preposition,** 44)
> The old house fell *down.* (**adverb,** 43)
> Adversity will never *down* Bob. (**verb,** 41)

The following are a few examples of the great number of words that may be commonly used as two or more parts of speech: *while, right, walk, rain, cry, play, paper, water, call, ground, land, stone, after, before, fast, outside, iron, last, paint, past, picnic, round, still, that, fly.*

Your dictionary will record the various meanings that a given word has developed in the course of its history as a word and will label the part of speech of its different meanings.

Exercise 2.1   Parts of Speech: A Diagnostic Lesson
Identify the part of speech for each of the words in boldface as it is used within its sentence.

>   *adverb*   *noun conj.*   *verb*
> EXAMPLE: Do you **always** have the proper **light when** you **study**?

a. **Plan** your **study** time **very** carefully.
b. The architect showed **us** her **plans** for the **school** building.
c. Do you **usually ride** to **school** on the bus, or do you walk?
d. **After** the long bus **ride,** he took a **walk** in the **park.**
e. He will **skillfully back** the car **down** the steep slope and **park** it.
f. She **often** went **back** to her **home** town **for** visits **after** she moved away.
g. **With** the money **from** his first novel **he** made a **down** payment on a new **home.**
h. **They** made three first **downs** in the **second** quarter **of** the football game.
i. I will **second** your motion **if** you **wish.**
j. **Ah,** my greatest **wish** is to see that very famous **painting**!

    k. Are you **painting** your house **this spring?**
    l. Every **one** of **you** should **spring** to your feet **and volunteer** to help.
    m. **Oh,** how **cold** the **spring** water tasted to the thirsty **volunteers!**
    n. She **stayed at** home **because she** had a **cold.**
    o. The **criminal** received a **stay** of execution.

NOUNS

53   There are two general classes of nouns: **common** and **proper.**

54   A **common noun** is the name that refers to a class or to anyone of a class of persons, places, or things:

    The *man* walked down the *street.*   The *cow* is a domestic *animal.*

55   A **proper noun** is the name of a particular person, place, or thing; and it should be capitalized:

    We are *Americans.*   *Jane* was born in *Alaska.*
    Apollo 15, with three astronauts, was launched on July 26, 1971.

    ♦ Some proper nouns have become the generic or class names of things and are not capitalized.

    We read about *ohms, volts,* and *amperes* in a book about electricity. (from Ohm, Volta, Ampére)

56   In addition to these general classes of nouns there are special classes: **abstract, concrete, collective, compound.**

    ♦ The **verbal noun,** though it is not in the strictest sense a pure noun, is very important. (See 61*d*, 61*e*, 200–268). It has some characteristics of both noun and verb, and it may in form be either an infinitive (199) or a gerund (200):

    Writing business letters is important work. (*Writing* is a gerund [200] used as subject of the sentence, but it retains verb force sufficiently to have *letters* as its object.)

    To *write* good letters requires skill. (To *write* is an infinitive [199] used as the subject of the sentence; *letters* is the object of the infinitive.)

57   An **abstract noun** is a noun that names a quality or attribute:

    We like *honesty* and *courtesy.*

58   A **concrete noun** is a noun that names something in its material form:

    A *telephone* is on the *desk.*

59   A **collective noun** is a noun that is singular in form but names a group or collection (92, 240):

Our *school* has a strong football *team.*

60 A **compound noun** is a noun made up of two or more words. Some compounds are written as separate words, some are hyphenated, and others are written solid as one word: *fountain pen, maple syrup; secretary-general, father-in-law; fireplace, newspaper.*

The only safe guide for determining the correct form of a compound is the dictionary.

♦ Some grammarians classify such nouns as *Duke of Wellington* and *Chase Manhattan Bank* as **phrasal nouns**.

61 There are many **noun equivalents** (substantives, 47), such as the following:

  a. **Pronoun** (40): *She* is my teacher.
  b. **Adjective** (42): The *young* are full of energy.
  c. **Adverb** (43): Since *then* I haven't seen him.
  d. **Gerund** (200): *Walking* is good exercise.
  e. **Infinitive** (199): *To win* is not our real intention.
  f. **Phrase** (8): *Over the top* is our aim.
  g. **Clause** (9, 396, 399): *That he has gone* is a fact.
  h. **Quotation** (507): *"The time has arrived,"* the speaker said.

62 The **modifications** of nouns are **gender, person, number,** and **case.**

63 **Gender** is distinction as to sex; therefore there are logically but two classes of gender. However, the following four are described by many grammarians; **masculine, feminine, neuter, common.**

64 A noun which denotes a **male** is of the **masculine gender:** *man, boy, father, brother.*

65 A noun which denotes a **female** is of the **feminine gender:** *woman, girl, mother, sister.*

66 A noun which names an object without **sex** is of the **neuter gender:** *book, rock, desk, house.*

67 Nouns which may denote either male or female or both are said to be of **common gender:** *student, child, singers, teachers.*

68 There are three ways of indicating gender:

  a. Change of word: *man—woman, rooster—hen.*
  b. Addition of a descriptive word: *salesman—saleswoman.*
  c. Use of a suffix: *host—hostess, hero—heroine.*

♦ There is a tendency to avoid making gender distinctions when they are not essential, for example, *host—hostess.*

69   **Person** denotes the speaker, the person or thing spoken to, the person or thing spoken of. There are three classes: **first, second, third.**

   Nouns used alone are always in the third person. When a noun is used in apposition to a pronoun, the pronoun determines the person of the verb.

70   The **first person** denotes the person speaking:

   I, Fred Smith, am willing to go.

71   The **second person** denotes the person or thing spoken to:

   You, Lola, are selected for the honor.

72   The **third person** denotes the person or thing spoken of:

   Our *coach* is here now; *she* will help us.

73   **Number** shows whether the noun refers to one or to more than one person, place, or thing. There are two classes: **singular, plural.**

74   **Singular number** denotes one: *tree, desk, book.*

75   **Plural number** denotes more than one: *trees, desks, books.*

Plurals of Nouns

   The dictionary is the only complete guide in forming plurals.

76   Form the plurals of **most nouns** including those **ending in silent e,** by adding *s* to the singular: *bird—birds, tree—trees, tube—tubes.*

77   Form the plurals of nouns **ending in s, ss, x, z, zz, ch, tch, sh** by adding *es* to the singular: *gas—gases, guess—guesses, box—boxes, fez—fezes, buzz—buzzes, church—churches, ditch—ditches, bush—bushes.*

78   Form the plurals of most nouns **ending in o preceded by a consonant** by adding *es* to the singular: *hero—heroes, potato—potatoes.*

   Some exceptions to this rule are: *piano—pianos, solo—solos.*

79   Form the plurals of nouns **ending in o preceded by a vowel** (vowels are *a, e, i, o, u,* and sometimes *w* and *y*) by adding *s* to the singular: *radio—radios, trio—trios, two—twos.*

   The plurals of a few nouns **ending in o** are formed by adding either *s* or *es* to the singular, but *es* is usually preferred: *volcano—volcanoes—volcanos, zero—zeroes (or zeros).*

80   Form the plurals of **common nouns ending in y preceded by a consonant** by changing *y* to *i* and adding *es: cry—cries, sky—skies.*

   Form the plurals of all **proper nouns ending in y** by adding *s:*

We went to the party with the *Kellys*. Three *Henrys* and two *Marys* were there.

81 Form the plurals of nouns **ending in y preceded by a, e, o, u** by adding only *s*: *day–days, turkey–turkeys, buoy–buoys, guy–guys*.

82 Form the plurals of some nouns **ending in f or fe** by changing the *f* or *fe* to *v* and adding *es*: *sheaf–sheaves, wife–wives, half–halves*.

Other examples are *calf, elf, leaf, life, self, knife, loaf, thief, shelf, wolf*.

83 Form the plurals of other nouns **ending in f or fe** by adding only *s*: *fife–fifes, roof–roofs*.

Other examples are *belief, chief, gulf, grief, safe, strife, cliff, proof*.

84 Form the plural of some nouns **by changing vowels** within them: *goose–geese, foot–feet, man–men, woman–women*. Note: *mouse–mice*.

85 Form the plurals of these two nouns by adding *en* or *ren*: *ox–oxen, child–children*.

86 The plurals of **compound nouns** (60) are usually formed by adding *s* or *es* to the main word of the compound; but the plurals of some are formed by adding *s* at the end, and for others the first part of the word is pluralized; in a few cases both words are pluralized: *father-in-law–fathers-in-law, suitcase–suitcases*.

87 Form the plurals of nouns **ending in ful** by adding *s* at the end. Do not make the mistake of placing the *s* before the last syllable.

She used three *spoonfuls* (not *spoonsful*) of sugar.

88 Form the plurals of letters, symbols, figures, and words regarded as words by adding *'s*, or sometimes just *s*:

Dot your *i's*, cross your *t's*, and make your *3's* (or *3s*) plainer.
You have too many *and's* (or *ands*) in this sentence.
It happened in the *1890's* (or *1890s*).

89 Some nouns have the same form in both numbers: *deer, sheep, trout*.

90 Some nouns are plural in form but singular in use: *measles, mumps, ethics, news, summons*.

91 A few nouns are used in the plural only: *scissors, tongs, trousers*.

92 **Collective nouns** are singular when the group is considered a unit, but plural when the individuals are indicated:

The *team* (as a unit) built *its* reputation on honesty.
The *class* (as individuals) have received *their* diplomas.

93 Some foreign words retain their original foreign plurals: *crisis–crises, axis–axes, thesis–theses, cactus–cacti, alumna–alumnae*.

Exercise   2.2   Writing Plurals.
Form the correct plural for each of the following:

story	baby	church
elf	alumnus	grocery
Mary	child	mouse
turkey	potato	3
tooth	thief	tomato
piano	spoonful	knife
bench	valley	country
berry	roof	man
handful	woman	jockey
trout	radio	safe
w	leaf	bunch
scissors	moose	runner-up
pony	father-in-law	
chief	handkerchief	

Noun Case: Uses of the Nominative Case

94   The **case** of a noun or pronoun shows its relation to other words in the sentence.   There are three cases: **nominative, possessive,** and **objective,** but nouns show case change only in the possessive form.   The nominative and objective cases of nouns are used only descriptively now, but these terms help to explain grammatical terms such as *nominative absolute* and *adverbial objective.*

95   The **subject** of a finite verb, that is, one limited by number and person, is in the nominative case:

Mary wrote a book.   (A *finite* verb can be used as a predicate, while the *infinite* forms—infinitive, participle, and gerund—cannot be so used.)

96   The **predicate nominative** is in the nominative case:

George is my *friend.*
It was *she.*
She was made *captain.*   (289)

A noun or pronoun that completes the meaning of the predicate and denotes the same person or thing as the subject is a **predicate nominative** (sometimes called **subjective complement,** 179).

DIAGRAM—Sentence with a *noun predicate nominative* or *subjective complement:*

The girls were *students.*

DIAGRAM–Sentence with *compound predicate nominative* or *subjective complement:*

The trees are *cedars* and *maples.*

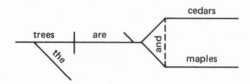

97   A **noun of direct address** is in the nominative case:

Tom, lend me your book.
Will you help me, *Tom,* with this problem?
When will we finish it, *Tom?*

♦ The noun of address is used to call the attention of the one spoken to. It is separated from the rest of the sentence by a comma or commas (500).

98   A noun used as an **exclamation** is in the nominative case: *Fire! Fire!*

99   The **nominative absolute** is a substantive (47, 61) used in an absolute construction:

The rain having ceased, we went home. (499)
The night being cold, I wore an overcoat.

♦ The absolute construction is a word or a phrase related to the thought of the sentence in which it is found, but not grammatically related to any word of the sentence. It is usually made up of a noun and a participle (201, 269), either with or without modifiers (7). The absolute construction is easily changed into a clause:

The work being completed, we went home.
The work completed, we went home. (*Being* is very frequently omitted in writing.)
When the work was completed, we went home. (**clause,** 9, 396)

The absolute construction is set off from the rest of the sentence by a comma (499). Never use a period for this purpose:

Incorrect: The work being completed. We went home.
Correct: The work being completed, we went home.

100   A substantive may be in the nominative case by **apposition:**

> Ms. Jones, *my teacher,* is in Chicago. (in apposition with the subject)
> That is Ms. Jones, *my teacher.* (in apposition with the predicate nominative)

The substantive used in apposition—**appositive**—differs from one used in the predicate nominative (96) in that it has no verb to connect it with the word which it explains. In the two illustrations given, *my teacher* is set off by commas and no verb is used to connect *teacher* with *Ms. Jones.*

DIAGRAM—Sentence with *noun in apposition with the subject:*

Miss Smith, the *teacher,* bought a book.

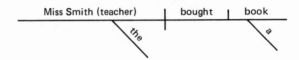

101   An **appositive** is a word, a phrase (393), or a clause (404–407) placed after a substantive (47) to explain it. In 100 the word *teacher* explains who *Ms. Jones* is. The appositive is nearly always in the same case as the word which it explains (but see 118), and it is usually set off by commas (500):

> Ms. Jones, my *teacher,* writes books. (**appositive word**)
> Mr. Barnes, *driving his car,* met us at the airport. (**appositive phrase**)
> The fact *that he is coming* makes us happy. (**appositive clause**)

Although the appositive is thought of usually as a substantive (47), a modifier may be used appositively. The adjective is frequently used appositively (277), just as it is often used in the predicate (278):

> The tree, *tall* and *beautiful,* stood near the lake. (*Tall* and *beautiful* are used appositively to explain the kind of tree.)
> The tree near the lake was *tall* and *beautiful.* (*Tall* and *beautiful* are used in the predicate, 289, to describe *tree,* and the linking verb *was,* 179, is used as a connective.)

Uses of the Objective Case

102   The **direct object** of a verb is in the objective case:

> Richard painted the *picture.*

The direct object is sometimes called the **object complement** (6, 174). It completes the predicate by naming the receiver of the action in the active voice (184).

103   The direct object of a verb is also said to be in the **accusative case,** but this term is now infrequently used in English terminology.

104 The **predicate objective**, or **objective complement** (180), may follow verbs of *making, naming, calling, choosing, appointing,* and would appear in the position after the **direct object**; the second object completes the meaning of the predicate and relates to the direct object.

We elected Laura *captain.*

105 The **indirect object** is in the objective case:

Mary gave *Alice* a book.

The **indirect object** may be changed into a prepositional phrase, which then follows the direct object:

Mary gave a book to *Alice.*

The preposition (44) used in forming such a phrase is either *to* or *for.*

DIAGRAM—Sentence with *indirect object:*

His mother gave the *boys* some cookies.

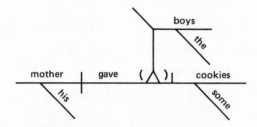

106 The **object of a preposition** is in the objective case:

The great plane flew over the *house.* (object of *over*)

107 The **adverbial objective** is a noun (with its modifiers) used as an adverb to express time, distance, measure, weight, or value. It may be modified by an adjective, such as *three* in the following example:

The child walked *three miles.*

108 The **subject of an infinitive** (199, 272) is in the objective case:

James believed the *teacher* to be his friend.
There is no need for the *students* to help.

109 The **complement** of the infinitive *to be* having a subject is in the objective case:

James believed the teacher to be *his friend.*
John thought her to be *me.* (272)

When the infinitive *to be* has no subject, the complement is in the nominative case:

Ann wishes to be the *villain* in the play.
He was thought to be *I.* (273)

110 The **direct object of an infinitive** is in the objective case:

Helen likes to paint *pictures*.   The judge tried to help *him*.

111 A substantive may be in the objective case by **apposition** (100, 101):

We admire Dr. Brown, our *physician.*
We heard from Mrs. Hill, our *principal.*

112 The **object of a participle** (201, 269) is in the objective case:

Waving his *hand,* the boy rode away.

113 The **object of a gerund** (200, 266) is in the objective case:

Playing *games* is fun.

114 The **cognate object** is in the objective case:

She ran a good *race.*

When the object of a verb expresses an idea similar to that of the verb itself, the object is called **cognate**:

He sleeps a peaceful *sleep.*   He fought a good *fight.*

115 The **retained object** is in the objective case:

I was given a *watch* by my father.

A retained object is one that has been retained after a verb has been changed from active (184) to passive (185) voice:

My father gave (active) me a *watch.* (direct object)
I was given (passive) a *watch* by my father. (retained object)
A watch was given *me* by my father. (retained object)

Note that either the direct or indirect object may be retained.

Exercise 2.3   Nouns as Parts of the Sentence.
For each noun in boldface indicate its use within the sentence (e.g., as subject, direct object, indirect object, predicate nominative, object of a preposition, or appositive).

                    subj.   pred. nom.
EXAMPLE: Leon's **hobby** is **chess.**

a. **Sid** made two **baskets** first.
b. Ted was **winner** of first **prize.**
c. Miss Heller, the **teacher**, gave **Harry** a **pen.**
d. The **sign** in the **window** fell.
e. He had been a **violinist** in **Paris.**
f. Did **Dick** take his **books** home?
g. Hand **Manuel** the **newspaper.**
h. **Rex** was no **pilot.**
i. Give **Steve** the **ticket.**

j. **Lisa** handed **Alice** her calculator.
k. For **bait** they used **worms.**
l. **Teresa** is a competitive **student.**
m. **Kristin** threw a ball to **Rowdy,** her **dog.**
n. Sara offered **Don** a good **job.**
o. There is a good **play** at the **theater.**
p. The main **event** will be an **exhibit.**
q. This is the **note** about the **party.**
r. Paul rowed the **boat,** an old **one,** to **shore.**
s. Todd is beside **Tim** at the **left.**
t. The speakers are **Eric** and **Carl,** my **brothers.**

Uses of Possessive Case

116 The **possessive case** denotes ownership, possession, or a similar relationship:

This is *Robert's* book.

♦ The possessive case is referred to as the **genitive case** by some grammarians.

117 The noun (or pronoun, 146) in the possessive case is used as a modifier, and as a modifier it is sometimes called a **possessive adjective** (127, 131, 146, 270, 281):

He found *Sylvia's book.* (*Sylvia's* modifies *book.*)
The *girl's* hair is brown. (*Girl's* modifies *hair.*)

118 A noun in the possessive case may be used as an appositive of another noun (100, 101):

Bob drives his brother *Harry's* car.

Notice that *brother* would have the possessive form (his *brother's* car) if the appositive were omitted.

119 Ownership or possession may be denoted by the noun in a phrase introduced by *of*:

the *poems of Keats*   the *music of Schubert*

This is the form most widely used with inanimate things:

The *leaves of the tree* (instead of the *tree's leaves*) are falling.

But many neuter nouns (66) are correctly used with the regular possessive form, although there is no ownership involved. Here are a few of these: *a week's work, a dime's worth, for pity's sake, heart's desire, yesterday's report, time's flight.*

Possessive Forms of Nouns

120 To form the possessive singular of a noun, use an apostrophe and *s* after the word (519): the *boy's* cap, the *girl's* book.

It is correct to use either the apostrophe alone or *'s* in forming the possessive singular of a proper noun ending in *s*:

He did this for *Jesus'* sake.   She carried *Chris's* book.

Form the possessive of a noun of two or more syllables ending in *s* or an *s*-sound and not accented on the last syllable by adding the apostrophe only in written form:

He did it for his *conscience'* sake.

121 Form the possessive of a plural noun that ends in *s* by adding the apostrophe only:

The two *boys'* caps are torn.
The three *students'* books are here.

122 To form the possessive of a plural noun not ending in *s*, add an apostrophe and *s:*

men's shoes, *oxen's* horns

123 In forming the possessive of a compound, place the possessive ending after the last word: *Queen of England's throne, sister-in-law's farm.*

The possessives of plurals of compounds (86) are formed in the same way:

brothers-in-law's farms

124 When two nouns are used to indicate common ownership, the sign of possession is placed after the second noun:

Smith and *Brown's* office (Smith and Brown occupy the same office.)

125 When two nouns are used to show separate ownership, add the sign of possession to both nouns:

Opal's and *Edna's* coats are the same color.

126 In such phrases as *nobody else,* the possessive is formed by placing the sign at the end of the phrase:

nobody else's business

127 A noun or pronoun introducing a gerund (200) is usually in the possessive case:

She told us of *Jane's* winning the prize.
He asked me about *my* writing the story.

Exercise 2.4   Writing Possessives.
For each of the following write its singular possessive form and its most com-

mon plural possessive form.

EXAMPLE: bird   bird's   birds'

donkey	puppy
dairy	attorney
son-in-law	child
workman	thief
elephant	sheep
deer	dog
teacher	boy
enemy	horse
goose	spy
student	friend
woman	wolf
hero	canary
fox	guest
ox	wife
veteran	self

PRONOUNS

128 A **pronoun** is a word that substitutes for a noun and that can be used in the same position in the sentence. The classes of pronouns include the following: **personal, interrogative, demonstrative** (138, 281), **indefinite** (139, 281), **possessive** (131). The last three are sometimes called **pronominal adjectives** (131, 140, 281) because they are used as adjectives when the substantive (47) is expressed.

129 The **antecedent** of a pronoun is the word for which the pronoun stands:

Mary brought her book. (*Mary* is the antecedent of *her*.)
The *person* who came here has gone. (The antecedent of *who* is *person*.)

130 A pronoun generally agrees with its antecedent in **gender, person,** and **number.** Its case is determined by its use in a particular group of words. Form modifications of the pronoun are the same as those of the noun: **gender, person, number,** and **case.**

131 An **absolute possessive pronoun** represents the possessor and the thing possessed. It does not modify a noun directly. The absolute possessive pronouns are *mine, yours, his, hers, its, theirs, ours.*

This book is *mine.* (The word *mine* here is equivalent to *my book;* therefore it represents both the possessor and the thing possessed.)

Some authorities classify as **possessive adjectives** (146) the forms *my, your, his, her, its, our, their,* when they are used as modifiers. However, these remain pronouns and agree with their antecedents in gender, person, and number, even when they modify nouns.

132   **Personal pronouns** show by their form whether they are the first, second, or third person (69–72). The simple personal pronouns include *I, you, he, she, it, we, they,* and their inflected forms (144).

133   **Compound personal pronouns** are formed by adding *-self* or *-selves* to some of the simple personal pronouns: *myself, yourself, himself, herself, itself, ourselves, themselves. (Hisself* and *theirselves* are incorrect forms.)

134   A compound personal pronoun is used correctly as a **reflexive pronoun** to refer an action to the subject of a sentence:

He helped himself.

It is also correctly used as an **intensive pronoun** in apposition for emphasis:

He himself is wrong.

A compound personal pronoun should not be used to take the place of a simple personal pronoun:

John and *I* (not *myself*) went to the show.

135   A **relative pronoun** is not only a pronoun but also a connecting word. It refers to a substantive (47) in the main clause (397) in which it is found, and it joins an adjective clause (408) to its antecedent. The relative pronoun has a use in the dependent clause (160, 398), such as subject, object of verb, or object of preposition, and it joins the dependent clause to an independent, or main, clause. Because the relative pronoun connects a subordinate clause with a main clause, it is called also a **conjunctive pronoun.** Words used as relative pronouns are *who, whom, whose, which, that,* and *what* (*what* has no antecedent and is equivalent to *that which*):

The boy *who* sang is here.   *What* was said is well known.

136   The **compound relative pronoun** is formed by adding *-ever* or *-soever* to certain simple relatives. The case of a relative pronoun depends on its use in its own clause:

We invite *whoever* will come.   (*Whoever* is the subject of *will come.*)

137   The **interrogative pronouns** are *who, whom, whose, which,* and *what,* when they are used in asking questions:

Who is the speaker?

138   The **demonstrative** or **adjective pronouns** (128, 139, 140, 290) point out particular persons, places, or things:

This is my pencil.   *That* is your book.

♦ The most commonly used demonstratives are *this, that, these,* and *those.* When one of these words modifies a substantive (47), it ceases to be a pronoun and becomes an adjective (140, 275, 281, 290):

That is a beautiful tree. **(pronoun)**   *That* tree is beautiful. **(adjective)**

139 **Indefinite pronouns** point out persons, places, or things less specifically than demonstratives do (138):

All did their work.   *Many* were absent today.

♦ Some of the commonly used indefinites are *everybody, everyone, anybody, nobody, each, either, neither, one, none, some, other, another, few, all, many, several,* and *both.* When one of these words modifies a substantive (47), it ceases to be a pronoun (128) and becomes an adjective (140, 275, 281, 290):

Many attended the lecture today. **(pronoun)**
Many students attended the lecture today. **(adjective)**
Some do not like this story. **(pronoun)**
Some students do not like this story. **(adjective)**

140 Words that are sometimes used as adjectives and sometimes as pronouns are often called **pronominal adjectives** or **adjective pronouns** (128, 138, 139, 281):

Several people did their duty.   *Several* did their duty.

141 In using relative pronouns (135), *who* is generally used to refer to persons; *which,* to animals and things; and *that,* to either persons, animals, places, or things:

It was a woman *who* helped us.
The dog, *which* is a faithful animal, is loved by the family.
He spoke of the sailors and the ships *that* were lost.

♦ With clauses that are nonrestrictive or defining, *who* or *which* is used; but with clauses that are restrictive or limiting, *that* is used by careful writers.

142 Make the pronoun agree with its antecedent (129) in number (73):

Each boy should study *his* (not *their*) lesson. (*Boy* is singular and calls for a singular pronoun.)

Exercise 2.5   Kinds of Pronouns.
Classify each of the pronouns printed in boldface as *personal, demonstrative, indefinite,* or *relative.*

                    Indef.   *Personal*
EXAMPLE: **Many** are careless when **they** drive.

a. If you respect **yourself**, you respect **others**.
b. If **you** are courteous, you will receive the respect of **those** about you.
c. Are **you** sure that your manners are as **they** should be?
d. **Many** are more thoughtless than **they** realize.
e. **Some** offend **everybody whom** they meet through mere carelessness.

   f. **She who** has rude manners shows that **she** is thoughtless.
   g. Courtesy wins respect for **her who** practices it.
   h. We should treat with respect **those** who serve **us**.
   i. When others respect **you**, you respect **yourself**.
   j. Courtesy expresses **itself** alike to **all**.
   k. **Those** who are rude to servants show that **they** are unrefined.
   l. If **you** are courteous, you will respect **everyone**.
   m. **Those who** are late to appointments show that **they** are careless.
   n. **Those** late for appointments show that **they** lack courtesy.
   o. Good citizens are **they** who respect **those** about them.
   p. Do you respect all **whom you** meet?
   q. Do **you** win the respect of **those** about you?
   r. There are **many who** hurt **themselves** by their rudeness.
   s. Were you ever proud of **yourself** when **you** were rude?
   t. Time is valuable; **you** should not waste **it**.

Case: Forms and Use of Pronouns

143   The case forms of pronouns are always determined by their own use in a sentence, never by the use of their antecedent.

   Was it he *whom* they saw? (*Whom* is the object of *saw*.)

144   The nominative case forms of the personal pronouns are *I, we, he, she, they;* the objective case forms are *me, us, him, her, them*. The forms *it* and *you* are used in both the nominative and objective case. *Her* may be either objective or possessive.

Declension of Personal Pronouns

	SINGULAR			PLURAL		
	Nomina- tive	Possessive	Objec- tive	Nomina- tive	Possessive	Objec- tive
1ST PER.	I	my, mine	me	we	our, ours	us
2ND PER.	you	your, yours	you	you	your, yours	you
3RD PER.	he	his	him	they	their, theirs	them
	she	her, hers	her	they	their, theirs	them
	it	its	it	they	their, theirs	them

145   Personal pronouns (132) in the nominative case have the same uses as nouns (95-101), as follows:

   a. **Subject of a verb:** *I* went home.
   b. **Predicate nominative:** I am *he.*
   c. **Direct address:** *You,* Fred, can give a demonstration.
   d. **Exclamation:** Lucky *you!*

    e. **Nominative absolute:** *He* being ill, we did not go.

    f. **Appositive:** We, Mary and *I*, played ball.

    g. **Complement of the infinitive *to be* not having a subject:** John was thought to be *I*. (See 109, 274.)

146 Personal pronouns (132) in the possessive case **do not require the sign of possession** as do nouns. The possessive forms (see 131, 144) are *my, mine, our, ours, his, her, hers, their, theirs, its, your, yours:*

> That book is *yours.* (not *your's*)

The only correct use of the apostrophe with the personal pronoun is in contractions which are often found in reported speech, but less frequently in formal written text.

> It's time to go home.   They're ready to see you.

The following pronouns in the possessive case are sometimes called **possessive adjectives:** *my, your, his, her, its, our, their.* (131, 281)

147 Personal pronouns in the **objective case** (144) may be used in these ways:

    a. **Direct object of a verb:** The teacher praised *her.*

    b. **Indirect object:** He gave *her* a copy of the essay.

    c. **Object of a preposition:** I spoke to *him.*

    d. **Subject of an infinitive:** He asked *me* to say.

    e. **Complement of the infinitive *to be* having a subject:** Did you think Sally to be *her?* (109, 273)

    f. **Object of a participle:** Seeing *me* at the door, my aunt smiled happily.

    g. **Object of an infinitive:** Mary tried to help *me.* (110)

    h. **Object of a gerund:** Helping *him* was my duty. (113, 200, 266)

    i. **Appositive:** Ann invited us, Bill and *me.*

148 A noun or pronoun following *than* or *as* is in the nominative or objective case according to its construction in the elliptical (5) clause to which it refers:

> You are stronger than *he* (is strong).
> You like her better than (you like) *me.*
> Tony is not as strong as *you* (are strong).
> Tony likes him as well as *you* (do).

149 When a subject or a predicate nominative is compound (17, 96), both parts should be in the nominative case form:

> John and *he* are going.
> The winners are Bill and *she.*

150 Do not repeat a subject by using a pronoun after it:

> *Charles* (not *Charles he*) studied hard.

151 When a pronoun is used as the subject or as a predicate nominative and has a noun in apposition (100, 101) following it, the nominative form (144) of the pronoun should be used:

> All *we* students went to the play.
> It was *we* girls who did the work.

152 A personal pronoun used as a **predicate nominative** should be in nominative case form (144, 180):

> The guests were *she* (not *her*) and *they* (not *them*).

♦ Some authorities feel that "It is *me*" is natural and acceptable in colloquial speech, but careful writers prefer "It is *I*" in formal written work.

153 If a pronoun appears in the **compound object** of a **verb** or of a **preposition**, the pronoun should be in the objective case form:

> Our uncle saw Clyde and *me*.   The woman spoke to Grace and *me*.

154 When the **indirect object** (105) is compound, all pronoun parts should be in the objective case form:

> The farmer gave *her* and *me* some apples.

155 When a pronoun is the direct (147*a*) or the indirect (147*b*) object of a verb and has a noun in apposition (101), use the objective form of the pronoun:

> Our teacher saw *us* girls.   Bob sent *us* boys a message.

156 *But,* when used in the sense of *except,* is a preposition (341) and must, like *except* and *between,* have an object:

> I invited all the girls but *her*.   He stood between you and *me*.

157 When a pronoun is the object of a preposition (147*c*) and has with it a noun in apposition (101), use the objective form of the pronoun:

> Sue came with *us* students.

158 *Who, whom, whose, which,* and *what* are **interrogative pronouns** when they are used in asking questions.

159 *Who,* whether interrogative or relative, is the nominative case form:

> *Who* did Wilma say was the speaker? (*Who* is the subject of *was*; the clause *who was the speaker* is the object of *say*.)

Whom is the objective case form:

> *Whom* will you send to town?
> I met the girl of *whom* you spoke. **(relative)**

Declension of Relative Pronouns

Nominative	SINGULAR AND PLURAL Possessive	Objective
who	whose	whom
which	whose	which

160 The case form of the pronoun used as a relative (135) depends upon the use of the relative in the clause (9) it introduces:

This is the boy *who* lost his book. (*Who* is subject of *lost.*)
The man *whom* you saw is my friend. (*Whom* is object of *saw.*)

161 The compound relative *whoever* is the nominative case form:

Stop *whoever* comes this way. (*Whoever* is the subject of *comes.* The clause *whoever comes this way* is the object of *stop.*)

162 The compound relative *whomever* is the objective case form:

Send it to *whomever* you choose. (*Whomever* is the object of *choose.* The clause *whomever you choose* is the object of the preposition *to.*)
Whomever you ask will be invited. (*Whomever* is the object of *ask.* The clause *whomever you ask* is the subject of the verb *will be invited.*)

♦ The case forms of the compound relative *whoever* seem more easily confused than the forms of *who.* When the compound relatives are used, the form may be determined more readily if words are supplied to show an antecedent. In 161, for example, the sentence would be expanded to *You stop him who comes this way.* The example in this section would be *He whom you ask will be invited.*

Exercise 2.6   Case of Pronouns.
Select the correct pronoun from each of the groupings in the following sentences. Indicate for each the use it has within the sentence (e.g., *subject, direct object, possessive,* etc.) and its case (*nominative, objective,* or *possessive*).

EXAMPLE: **Its/It's** time to go. <u>It's—subject, nominative.</u>
The team won **its/it's** game. <u>its—possessive, possessive.</u>

a. We met **he/him** on the street.
b. I handed **her/she** the book.
c. This chalk is **hers/her's.**
d. **It/It's** a very interesting book.
e. Isn't **she/her** a smart girl?
f. Was it **he/him who/whom** you saw?
g. They waved to **we/us** from the bus.
h. The overturned car lay on **its/it's** side in the field.
i. The house on the south side of the street is **our's/ours.**
j. It was **she/her who/whom** told us.
k. Max showed **we/us** his latest painting.
l. Others are glad when **you're/your** on time.
m. Mr. Doyle spoke to **they/them** about the meeting.
n. **They're/Their** always prompt.
o. If **its/it's** the right thing to do, do it.
p. Others judge you by **you're/your** manners.

q. The teacher gave **him/he** a good report.
r. It could have been **them/they** who wrote the letter.
s. Everyone enjoys **his'/his** witty remarks.
t. What is **you're/your** answer to the question?

Number

163   The **indefinite pronouns** *each, either, neither, one, everyone, anyone, some-one, no one, nobody, anybody, somebody, everybody* are singular (242):

Each girl should do *her* best.   Neither boy could sing *his* song.

Sometimes the meaning is so clearly plural that a singular personal pronoun cannot be used to refer to the indefinite pronoun:

Everyone was so busy writing a version of the story that *they* did not notice who had come in. (Not *he* did not notice.)

♦ **Current informal usage permits use of the plural with various indefinite pronouns.**

164   A pronoun must be singular when it refers to a noun modified by such indefinite adjectives (139, 140) as *each, every*, and *neither:*

Each boy brought *his* ticket.   Every girl brought *her* books.

165   A pronoun that refers to a collective noun (59) is singular if the group acts as a unit:

The band has won fame because of *its* leader.

But the pronoun is plural if the individuals of the group act as individuals:

The band have ordered *their* new instruments.

Usage

166   Most experts agree that *which* should not be used to refer to a complete statement (376):

Questionable: He had to work, *which* caused him to be late.
Better: He was late *because* he had to work.

167   The word *same* should not be used as a pronoun instead of *it* or *them:*

I have read your offer (offers) and have decided to accept it (*them*) (not *same* or *the same*).

168   *Them* is never used as an adjective nor as the subject of a sentence:

Those (not *Them* or *Them there*) books are mine.

169 *They* should not be used with indefinite reference:

People (not *They*) say that he is talented.

Exercise 2.7   Agreement of Pronoun and Antecedent.
Select the correct pronoun from each of the groupings of the following sentences.

a. If any man is late, **they/he** will not be admitted to the meeting.
b. Did each of the boys work by **himself/hisself**?
c. Each woman should feel that **her/their** job is important.
d. If either boy wants this apple, I'll give it to **them/him**.
e. Mary brought Jane and **me/myself** a book.
f. Either of those girls would do **her/their** work well.
g. Every girl tried to make **her/their** report interesting.
h. Can't each of the girls make **her/their** own bookshelf.
i. The jury finally reached **their/its** decision.
j. The boys really have no one to blame except **theirselves/themselves**.
k. Did every man pay **their/his** dues?
l. Not one of the girls would admit that **she/they** had broken the window.
m. Jessie and **myself/I** were never consulted.
n. Tell every boy to bring **his/their** pencil.
o. Each of the boys offered **his/their** help.
p. Neither of the tardy children had washed **their/his** hands.
q. Has Harvey prepared **himself/hisself** for that particular job?
r. The class proved loyal to **its/their** sponsor.
s. Did either of the girls give **their/her** report?
t. Each of those books has **their/its** place.
u. One girl did not hand in **their/her** paper.
v. If one of those women wants to help us, **she/they** may plan the meeting.
w. Each of the girls promised that **they/she** would make some candy for the sale.
x. Does every woman know what **she/they** should do?
y. Did each of the girls earn **their/her** money?
z. Everyone had helped **hisself/himself** to nuts.
aa. Not one of the girls raised **their/her** voice.
bb. The team wore **their/its** new warm-up suits.
cc. Each woman has the right to give **her/their** opinion on the subject.
dd. If either man finds the lost purse, **they/he** will receive a reward.

VERBS

170 A **verb** (41) is a word that expresses action, being, or state of being. A verb may be formed by a group of words; such a group is called a **verb phrase** or a

phrasal verb (181, 391). According to the way in which they form their principal parts (202), verbs are divided into two classes: **regular** (weak) and **irregular** (strong).

171 A **regular** (weak) **verb** forms its past tense (193) and past participle (201) by adding *d, ed,* or *t* to the present tense (191): *hear–heard–heard, help–helped–helped, deal–dealt–dealt.*

172 An **irregular** (strong) **verb** usually forms its past tense and past participle by changing a vowel of the present (or infinitive, 199) form: *begin–began–begun.*

Sometimes a different word may be used for a principal part: *go–went–gone.*

Sometimes all the principal parts are the same: *set–set–set.*

Exercise 2.8   Principal Parts of Verbs.

The present-tense forms of forty high-frequency verbs are listed below. Copy each verb and beside it write its past-tense form and its past-participle form.

EXAMPLE: see *saw   seen*

do	grow	drive
come	write	sing
eat	wear	fall
go	swear	ring
begin	swing	flow
choose	dive	weave
give	sink	speak
run	bring	throw
take	drag	tear
freeze	fly	swim
know	draw	shake
blow	hide	steal
break	drink	burst
ride		

Transitive and Intransitive

173 According to use, verbs are classified as **transitive** or **intransitive**.

174 A **transitive verb** has a receiver of the action. When the actor is the subject (3), the receiver of the action is the object (6):

Bob *wrote* a letter. (*Bob* is the subject of the verb *wrote. Letter* is the receiver of the action.)

When the receiver of the action is the subject, the verb is in the passive voice (185) but remains transitive:

A letter *was written* by Bob. (*Letter* is the subject of the verb *was written.*

Bob is the object of the preposition *by*.)

♦ When the passive voice is used, the name of the actor may not be expressed:

Many letters *were written.*

175 An **intransitive verb** does not require a receiver of the action expressed in the meaning of the verb:

The eagle *flew* over the mountain.

176 Many verbs may be used as transitive in one sentence and as intransitive in another sentence:

She sings well. (**intransitive**)
She sings beautiful songs. (**transitive**)

177 Intransitive verbs are of two classes: **complete** and **linking.**

178 A **complete verb** is an intransitive verb which makes a meaningful statement without the help of any other word:

Birds *fly.*   Fish *swim.*   The horse *drinks.*   Children *play.*

179 A **linking verb,** sometimes called a **copulative verb**, is an intransitive verb that connects the subject with a predicate substantive (47) or a predicate adjective (289).

The predicate substantive following the linking verb, sometimes called the **predicate nominative** (96) or subjective complement, denotes the same person, place, or thing as the subject:

Browning was a great *poet.*   The woman became a *lawyer.*

♦ A noun or pronoun joined to a subject by a linking verb is in the nominative case (96, 145-52):

It is *he.*   That was *she.*

The adjective following the linking verb, sometimes called the **predicate adjective** (289), describes, limits, or points out the subject:

The apple looks *good.*   The roses are *beautiful.*

♦ The most commonly used linking verb is *be* in its various forms, such as *am, is, are* (206). Some other commonly used linking verbs are *seem, become, appear, prove, look, remain, feel, taste, smell, sound, turn, grow, stay, continue.*

180 A **verb complement** is the substantive (47) or adjective (42, 275) that follows a transitive or linking verb to complete the meaning of the verb. There are several classes of complements:

 a. **Direct object** (102, 174)

   b. **Predicate objective** (104, 174)
   c. **Predicate nominative** (96, 179)
   d. **Predicate adjective** (179, 278)

Exercise 2.9   Recognizing Transitive and Intransitive Verbs.
   List the verb in each of the following sentences, identifying it as *T* if the verb
   is transitive or *I* if the verb is intransitive.

   EXAMPLE: She told us a good story.   *told–T*

   a. Our teacher read "The Great Stone Face" to us.
   b. It is a story by Nataniel Hawthorne.
   c. Hawthorne wrote the story about Profile Mountain.
   d. It is in the White Mountains of New Hampshire.
   e. The mountains occupy the northern third of the state.
   f. People call the cliffs the "Old Man of the Mountain."
   g. They jut out in a profile of a man's face.
   h. Hawthorne used his imagination for the story.
   i. With it he made the region popular.
   j. Tourists come far to see the "Old Man."

Exercise 2.10   Transitive and Intransitive Verbs.
   List the verbs in each of the following sentences. Classify each one as *T* if
   transitive, *IC* if intransitive complete, or *IL* if intransitive linking.

   a. Americans today honor Benjamin Franklin because he was a public-spirited
       and patriotic citizen.
   b. As a youth he lived in Boston, where his father was a soapmaker.
   c. Although Ben went to school for only two years, he read books avidly
       and so educated himself.
   d. At twelve he became an apprentice of his brother and wrote articles for
       his newspaper.
   e. When his brother grew jealous of him, the two quarreled, and Ben ran
       away to Philadelphia.
   f. There, while he was still quite young, he became the owner of his own
       printing shop.
   g. He bought several newspapers and published *Poor Richard's Almanac,*
       which is famous for its wisdom and wit.
   h. As his business prospered, he gave more time to public affairs.
   i. In 1757 he sailed for England, where he served as spokesman for the
       American colonies.
   j. Later he signed the Declaration of Independence, and for a time he con-
       ducted the postal service of the colonies.
   k. Then he was sent to France by the Continental Congress as our ambas-
       sador.
   l. Franklin was also a member of the commission which negotiated the

peace treaty at the end of the war, and he was a delegate to the Constitutional Convention.

Auxiliary Verbs

181   An **auxiliary verb** is a verb that aids or helps another verb express various shades of meaning. A verb with its helper or helpers is a **verb phrase** (41, 391). Some verbs used as auxiliaries are *do* (*did*), *be* (*am, is, are, was, were*), *have* (*has, had*), *may* (*might*), *can* (*could*), *must, will, shall* (*would, should*). Some of these verbs serve not only as auxiliaries but also as main verbs:

Jack *did* bring his book. (**auxiliary**)
Jack *did* good work. (**main verb**)

182   Although the linking verb *be* (179) **does not take an object,** all the forms of this verb may become auxiliaries in transitive verb phrases (174):

It *is* she. (**linking**)
Ruth *is* writing a letter. (*Is* is an **auxiliary** used in forming the verb phrase *is writing; write* is a transitive verb with the object *letter*.)

The forms of *be* are used also as auxiliaries in forming the passive voice (185).

The house *was* destroyed by fire.
The report *has been* received.

183   The modifications of a verb indicate its **voice, mood, tense, person,** and **number.**

Exercise 2.11   Recognizing Verbs and Verb Phrases.
On a separate sheet list the verb or verb phrase for each of the following sentences. Be sure to indicate the complete verb phrase, including any auxiliary verbs.

a.   American writers have given us some delightful stories of our own country.
b.   No American author has written more entertainingly than Washington Irving.
c.   In some of his stories he has given beautiful descriptions.
d.   As a boy, he frequently rambled through the neighboring countryside.
e.   He dearly loved its wooded hills.
f.   He wrote quite often about Sleepy Hollow.
g.   Because of his stories this region has become a land of romance.
h.   Some of the delightful characters of his stories will live for all time.
i.   At least two of these characters have become familiar to millions of people.
j.   Surely, few in America are unfamiliar with Ichabod Crane and Rip Van Winkle.

Voice

184 The **voice** of a verb indicates whether the subject of the verb acts or is acted upon. **Active voice** denotes that the subject of the verb is the actor:

The man *called* the dog.

185 **Passive voice** denotes that the subject receives the action:

The dog *was called* by the man.

The passive is always a verb phrase (41, 181, 391) composed of a form of the auxiliary (181, 208) *be* followed by a past participle (201, 208):

The letter *has been written* by the manager.

♦ Passive verbs sometimes have two receivers of the action: the subject and the retained object (115):

She was given a *scholarship.*

Exercise 2.12   Active or Passive Voice.

Copy the following sentences on a separate sheet, drawing one line under the simple subject of each sentence and two lines under the simple predicate. If the subject names the doer of the action, write **A** after the sentence to indicate active voice; if the subject names the receiver of the action, write **P** to indicate passive voice.

EXAMPLE: The <u>club</u> <u><u>was organized</u></u> by our singing coach.—**P.**

  a. The program was planned by an entertainment committee.
  b. The committee is appointed by the music students.
  c. Everyone had offered suggestions for the program.
  d. Many musical pieces were given by the members.
  e. The program was planned for its general appeal.
  f. Jazz moves nearly everyone.
  g. Two solos were omitted from the program.
  h. Both soloists were delayed by a traffic jam.
  i. The chorus sang two songs.
  j. After the intermission a boys' quartet entertained us with a medley.

Exercise 2.13

Rewrite each of the sentences in Exercise 2.12, changing the voice of the verb from active to passive or from passive to active.

EXAMPLE: The club was organized by our singing coach.
               <u>The singing coach organized our club</u>.

Mood

186 **Mood** (or **mode**) indicates the manner in which the action is conceived.

187   The **indicative mood** makes a statement of fact or asks a question:

He *is* my friend.   *Is* she a teacher?

188   The **imperative mood** gives a command or makes a request:

Shut the door.
Will you please *return* the book. (Note that a question mark is not used.)

189   The **subjunctive mood** expresses a doubt, a wish, a prayer, or a condition contrary to fact:

I wonder if it *be* true.   Peace *be* with you!
I wish I *were* a lawyer.   If I *were* you, I should go.

The **present subjunctive** occurs after verbs like *demand* (259):

I insist that he *go.*

Tense

190   **Tense** denotes the time of the action indicated by a verb. The time is not always the same as that indicated by the name of the tense.

191   The **present tense** may express action which is going on at the present time or which occurs always, repeatedly, or habitually:

The boys *are* ready to leave now.
They *go* by bus to school.
She *eats* cereal for breakfast.

The present tense may express future time:

The train *leaves* in five minutes.

It may be used as an historical present, referring to an event completed in past time.

The detective *solves* the mystery just in time.

192   The **present perfect tense** expresses action completed at the present time or continuing into the present:

He *has written* a letter to his uncle. (**completed**)
I *have lived* here for many years. (**continuing**)

193   The **past tense** expresses action completed at a definite time in the past:

He *wrote* the letter yesterday.

Do not use the emphatic past tense for the present perfect:

Joe *has* (not *did*) not come yet.

194   The **past perfect tense** expresses action completed before a stated or known time in the past:

He *had written* the letter before I saw him.

195   The **future tense** expresses action which will take place in the future:

He *will write* the letter tomorrow.

196   The **future perfect tense** expresses action which will be completed before a stated or known time in the future:

He *will have written* the letter before we arrive tomorrow.

197   A verb as a rule agrees with its subject in person (69-72) and number (73-75). Failure to observe this rule causes many errors:

He *doesn't* (not *don't*) know what to do.

♦ See 236-249, 262, and other sections under "verb, agreement of verb and subject" in the Index.

Exercise 2.14   Verb Tenses.

For each of the following sentences indicate the verb and its tense.

EXAMPLE: The orchestra and band have begun plans for the festival.
            have begun–*present perfect*

a.   Surely the bell rang a long time ago.
b.   Joe will run in the mile race next Wednesday.
c.   The river has risen several feet within the last hour.
d.   They have sat there on that bench for more than an hour.
e.   Speak to Ms. Williams about the price of the tickets for the play.
f.   She will not have finished her story by this afternoon.
g.   Harold and I swam across Round Lake yesterday afternoon.
h.   The workers will have laid the last brick by tomorrow night.
i.   Don had not written his application letter at noon today.
j.   The jazz band will play for us at the dance tomorrow evening.

Exercise 2.15   Forming Tenses.

For each sentence write the correct form of the verb indicated in parentheses.

EXAMPLE: (**ring**–past perfect) The bell __*had rung*__ before I opened the door.

a.   (**dive**–past) The girls ____ into the deep end of the pool.
b.   (**see**–past) Barry _____ the Veterans' parade yesterday.
c.   (**lie**–past perfect) We _____on the grass to rest awhile.
d.   (**do**–past) Robert_____ his very best to win his race.
e.   (**come**–future perfect) Jack_____before ten o'clock tonight.
f.   (**swing**–past) My cousin _____ her bat carelessly.
g.   (**bring**–past) Neither boy_____his own pencil.
h.   (**do**–present perfect) Ann_____the work for us.

i.   (**drink**—present perfect) They ____ all the milk in the refrigerator.
j.   (**blow**—past) The wind ____ hard all day yesterday.
k.   (**know**—future) She ____ the results of her exam before lunch.
l.   (**lie**—past) The tramp ____ down in the shade of that linden tree.
m. (**eat**—past perfect) Toni ____ her lunch before we arrived.
n.   (**break**—past perfect) We heard that he ____ the school record.
o.   (**ring**—past perfect) Class started before the bell ____ .
p.   (**give**—past) My brother ____ me this sweater for Christmas.
q.   (**throw**—past perfect) Mrs. Young ____ the small fish back into the lake.
r.   (**lie**—present) That lazy kitten ____ on the couch every day.
s.   (**shake**—future perfect) Jim ____ the smaller rugs before he leaves.
t.   (**go**—past perfect) Catrina ____ when we arrived at her house.

The Verbals

198 There are three forms of the verb, called **verbals**, that are also used as other parts of speech: **infinitive**, **gerund**, and **participle**.

199 The **infinitive** (265) is the form of the verb usually preceded by *to* (see 232)— a function word used to indicate that the following word is an infinitive.

We like *to play* basketball.

The **present infinitive** is the same as the simple present-tense form of the verb, usually preceded by *to: to see, to go, to do.*

The **perfect infinitive** is formed by placing *to have* before the past participle (201): *to have seen, to have gone, to have done.*

200 The **gerund** (56, 266-268) is a **verbal noun** (56) ending in *ing.* The gerund may, like any verb, take an object and it may be modified by an adjective or an adverb. A gerund is sometimes referred to as a **participial noun**, as in reality it is a participle used as a noun. The gerund is the name of an action:

Trying is commendable. (*Trying* is the subject of the sentence.)

Don enjoys *reading* history. (*Reading* is the object of the verb *enjoys* and it has its own object *history.*)

Walking rapidly is good exercise. (The adverb *rapidly* modifies the gerund *walking.*)

201 A **participle** is a verbal (198) which has some of the properties of a verb and some of the properties of an adjective. It is used, as an adjective, to modify a noun or a pronoun; it may, as a verb, take an object:

The person *waving* the flag is Robert. (*Waving* modifies *person* as an adjective and takes an object *flag* as a verb.)

The **present participle** ends in *ing* and generally describes an action going on at the same time as some other action, but it sometimes refers to time preceding that of the verb used as predicate:

Sitting here, we see the parade.
Standing at the window, I saw the parade.

The present participle is used in progressive forms of the active voice (205 and 209).

The **past participle** generally indicates completed action.

The past participle of a regular verb (171) usually has the same form as the past tense (193), but the form of the past participle of the irregular verbs (172) show numerous changes in form (204).

This was a work *done* for others.
The terms *suggested* by the committee were fair.

The past participle form is always combined with *have, has,* and *had* to form the perfect tenses (192, 194, 196).

The **perfect participle** is formed of *having* and the past participle:

Having finished the work, the people went home.

Exercise 2.16   Recognizing Verbal Phrases.

From each of the sentences below copy as many complete verbal phrases as you can find (remembering that the complete phrases may also include objects and modifiers). Then underline just the verbals, and identify them as infinitives, gerunds, or participles.

EXAMPLE: After graduating from college, she decided to study law.

       a. graduating from college—gerund
       b. to study law—infinitive

a. One of the most recent outdoor sports to become popular is hang gliding.
b. Having developed an interest in botany, she has written a textbook used in the schools.
c. Taking exercise daily is a good way to maintain physical fitness.
d. To avoid a cold, he will wear heavy clothes on the hayride scheduled for Friday night.
e. Being present at the time, I could not help noticing his reaction.
f. Those students lacking a sense of responsibility will delay doing their homework.
g. When they heard the band blaring in the distance, the children began to jump up and down excitedly.
h. Participating in extracurricular activities is very worthwhile, but you should never fail to do your schoolwork.
i. Seizing the opportunity, she took advantage of the crowd by making a sales pitch.
j. One should avoid hurting the feelings of others and should resist a temptation to say unkind things.

k. The best way to avoid tooth decay is brushing one's teeth after each meal.
l. Joan's singing of "Summertime" delighted the audience attending the concert.
m. All those interested in the Boosters Club are urged to attend the meeting.
n. After arranging the china carefully, they sat down to admire it.
o. Turning the corner quickly, I saw someone hiding behind a house.
p. Before doing your homework, you should try to get a little exercise.
q. Before beginning the test, be sure to read the instructions carefully.
r. The candidate making a campaign speech wore a big hat.

Principal Parts

202 The principal parts of a verb are the first person (70) singular (74) of the present (191) indicative (187), the first person singular of the past (193) indicative, and the past participle (201):

I *go*—I *went*—I have *gone*.   I *see*—I *saw*—I have *seen*.

203 Do not confuse the principal parts of irregular verbs (172):

I *saw* (not *seen*) him yesterday.

204 PRINCIPAL PARTS OF THE IRREGULAR VERBS

The reference list that follows presents the variations in form that speakers and writers of English today will need to recognize; included in the list are some verbs of quite limited present use, but they have been included for their recognition as irregular forms. Whenever more than one form is shown, the first is the more commonly used. The numbered notes will indicate special uses or limitations in use; they are keyed to the list for reference.

Present Tense	Past Tense	Past Participle
abide	abided, abode	abode
—	—	accursed,[2] accurst
arise	arose	arisen
awake	awoke	awoke
be (am is)	was, were	been
bear (*bring forth*)	bore	born[3]
bear (*carry*)	bore	borne
beat	beat	beaten, beat
beget	begot	begotten
begin	began	begun
behold	beheld	beheld, beholden[1]
bend	bent	bent
bereave	bereaved, bereft	bereaved,[1] bereft
beseech	beseeched, besought	besought
bespeak	bespoke	bespoken
bet	bet, betted	bet
bid (*command*)	bade	bid

Present Tense	Past Tense	Past Participle
bid (*money*)	bid	bidden, bid
bind	bound	bound, bounden[1]
bite	bit	bit, bitten
bleed	bled	bled
blend	blended, blent	blended, blent
bless	blessed, blest	blessed,[2] blest
blow	blew	blown
break	broke	broken
breed	bred	bred
bring	brought	brought
build	built, builded	built, builded
burn	burned, burnt	burned, burnt
burst	burst	burst, bursted[1]
buy	bought	bought
cast	cast	cast
catch	caught	caught
chide	chided, chidden	chided, chidden
choose	chose	chosen
cleave (*split*)	clove, cleft	cloven,[1] cleft
cleave (*adhere*)	cleaved, clave[4]	cleaved
cling	clung	clung
clothe	clothed, clad	clothed, clad
come	came	come
cost	cost	cost
creep	crept	crept
crow	crowed, crew	crowed, crown[4]
curse	cursed	cursed, cursed[2]
cut	cut	cut
deal	dealt	dealt
dig	dug	dug
dip	dipped	dipped
dive	dived, dove	dived
do	did	done
draw	drew	drawn
dream	dreamed, dreamt	dreamed, dreamt
dress	dressed, drest	dressed, drest
drink	drank	drunk, drunken[1]
drive	drove	driven
drop	dropped	dropped
dwell	dwelt, dwelled	dwelt, dwelled
eat	ate	eaten
engrave	engraved	engraved, engraven[4]
fall	fell	fallen
feed	fed	fed
feel	felt	felt
fight	fought	fought
find	found	found
flee, fly	fled	fled

Present Tense	Past Tense	Past Participle
fling	flung	flung
fly	flew	flown
forbear	forbore	forborne
forbid	forbade, forbad	forbidden, forbid
forget	forgot	forgot, forgotten
forsake	forsook	forsaken
freeze	froze	frozen
freight	freighted	freighted, fraught[1]
get	got	got, gotten[6]
gild	gilded	gilded
gird	girded, girt	girded, girt
give	gave	given
go	went	gone
grave	graved	graved, graven[1]
grind	ground	ground
grow	grew	grown
hang (*suspend*)	hung, hanged	hung
hang (*execute*)	hanged, hung	hanged
have	had	had
hear	heard	heard
heave	heaved, hove[7]	heaved, hove
hew	hewed	hewn, hewed
hide	hid	hidden, hid
hit	hit	hit
hold	held	held
hurt	hurt	hurt
keep	kept	kept
kneel	knelt	knelt
knit	knitted, knit	knitted, knit
know	knew	known
lade[4]	laded	laden,[1] laded
lay	laid	laid
lead	led	led
lean	leaned, leant	leaned, leant
leap	leaped	leaped, leapt
learn	learned, learnt[8]	learned, learnt
leave	left	left
lend	lent	lent
let	let	let
lie (*position*)	lay	lain, lorn[1]
lie (*tell a falsehood*)	lied	lied
light (*set fire to*)	lighted, lit	lighted, lit
light (*descend*)	lighted, lit	lighted, lit
load	loaded	loaded, laden[1]
lose	lost	lost
make	made	made
mean	meant	meant
meet	met	met

Present Tense	Past Tense	Past Participle
melt	melted	melted, molten[1]
mow	mowed	mowed, mown
owe	owed, ought[4]	owed
—	ought[5]	own[5]
pay	paid	paid
pen (*confine*)	penned	penned, pent[1]
plead	pleaded, plead	pleaded, plead
prove	proved	proved, proven[1]
put	put	put
quit	quit, quitted	quit, quitted
read	read	read
rend	rent	rent
rid	rid, ridden	rid, ridden
ride	rode	ridden
ring	rang	rung
rise	rose	risen
roast	roasted	roasted, roast[1]
run	ran	run
saw	sawed	sawed, sawn
say	said	said
see	saw	seen
seek	sought	sought
seethe	seethed, sod[4]	seethed, sod,[4] sodden[1]
sell	sold	sold
send	sent	sent
sew	sewed	sewed, sewn
shake	shook	shaken
shape	shaped	shaped, shapen[1]
shave	shaved	shaved, shaven[1]
shear	sheared, shore	sheared, shorn
shed	shedded	shed
shine	shone	shone
shoe	shod	shod
shoot	shot	shot
show	showed	shown, showed
shred	shredded, shred	shredded, shred
shrink	shrank, shrunk	shrunk, shrunken
shrive	shrived	shrived, shriven
shut	shut	shut
sing	sang, sung	sung
sink	sank, sunk	sunk, sunken[1]
sit	sat	sat
slay	slew	slain
sleep	slept	slept
slide	slid	slid, slidden
sling	slung	slung
slink	slunk	slunk
slit	slit	slit

Present Tense	Past Tense	Past Participle
smell	smelled, smelt	smelled, smelt
smite	smote	smitten
sow	sowed	sown, sowed
speak	spoke	spoken
speed	sped	sped
speed	speeded	speeded
spell	spelled, spelt	spelled, spelt
spill	spilled, spilt	spilled, spilt
spin	spun, span	spun
spit	spat, spit	spat, spit
split	split	split
spoil	spoiled, spoilt	spoiled, spoilt
spread	spread	spread
spring	sprang	sprung
stand	stood	stood
stay	stayed, staid	stayed, staid
stave	staved, stove	staved, stove
steal	stole	stolen
stick	stuck	stuck
stink	stank, stunk	stunk
strew	strewed	strewed, strewn
stride	strode	stridden
strike	struck	struck, stricken[1]
string	strung	strung
strive	strove	striven
sting	stung	stung
swear	swore	sworn
sweat	sweat, sweated,	sweat, sweated
sweep	swept	swept
swell	swelled	swelled, swollen
swim	swam	swum
swing	swung	swung
take	took	taken
teach	taught	taught
tear	tore	torn
tell	told	told
think	thought	thought
thrive	thrived, throve	thrived, thriven
throw	threw	thrown
thrust	thrust	thrust
toss	tossed, tost	tossed, tost
tread	trod	trodden, trod
wake	woke, waked	woke, waked, woken
wash	washed	washed, washen[4]
wax (*grow*)	waxed	waxed
wear	wore	worn
weave	wove	woven, weaved
wed	wed, wedded	wed, wedded

Present Tense	Past Tense	Past Participle
weep	wept	wept
wet	wet, wetted	wet, wetted
win	won	won
wind (*twist*)	wound	wound
wind (*sound*)	wound	wound, winded
(won)[4] (*accustomed*)	–	wont,[1] wonted[1]
wont[4] (*need to*)	wonted, wont	–
work	worked, wrought	worked, wrought
wring	wrung	wrung
write	wrote	written
writhe	writhed	writhed, writhen[4]

[1] The following participles are now used only as adjectives: I am *beholden* to you; the *bereaved* father; his *bounden* duty; a *bursted* bubble; a *cloven* foot; *fraught* with danger; a *graven* image; a *drunken* driver; heavily *laden* ships; now used only in *forlorn; molten* gold; *pent*-up anger; a *proven* case; *roast beef;* ill-*shapen;* a clean *shaven* face; a *sodden* meadow; a *sunken* garden; *stricken* by disease; *wont* to act with spirit (rare); in his *wonted* style (rare).

[2] Used as in [1] above, but notice the shift in word stress in their pronunciation as adjectives: *accurséd, curséd, blesséd, belovéd, learnéd.*

[3] Now used only in phrases such as: *born* into this world; *born* in bondage.

[4] Obsolete or archaic and no longer in use: *clave, engraven, lade, ought* (as the past tense of *owe*); *washen, writhen; won* and *wont* (as the present tense); *crown, sod.*

[5] *Ought* is an old past form of *owe,* replaced now by *owed; ought* is now used in a present sense, you *ought* to do it. *Own* is now used as an adjective, his *own* book.

[6] *Got* is the regular past form, with *got* or *gotten* as the past participle in standard English. In formal writing, *got* is preferred in the meaning of *possess* or *have.* In spoken English, *got* and *gotten* are equally used in the sense of *acquire* or *become.*

[7] Said principally of ships; the vessel *hove* in sight.

[8] A number of verbs show two past forms, one in *-ed,* the other in *-t* as in *learned, learnt.* In writing the *-ed* form is preferred, while in speaking the *-t* form is very widely heard.

Conjugation

205 The **conjugation** of a verb is the orderly arrangement of its forms through its voices (184–185), moods (186–189), tenses (190–196), persons (69–72, 197), and numbers (73–75, 197).

206 CONJUGATION OF THE VERB *BE*

INDICATIVE MOOD	**Singular**	**Plural**
Present Tense	1. I am 2. you are 3. he is	1. we are 2. you are 3. they are
Past Tense	1. I was 2. you were 3. he was	1. we were 2. you were 3. they were
Future Tense	1. I shall be 2. you will be 3. he will be	1. we shall be 2. you will be 3. they will be
Present Perfect Tense	1. I have been 2. you have been 3. he has been	1. we have been 2. you have been 3. they have been
Past Perfect Tense	1. I had been 2. you had been 3. he had been	1. we had been 2. you had been 3. they had been
Future Perfect Tense	1. I shall have been 2. you will have been 3. he will have been	1. we shall have been 2. you will have been 3. they will have been

SUBJUNCTIVE MOOD		
Present Tense	1. I be 2. you be 3. he be	1. we be 2. you be 3. they be
Past Tense	1. I were 2. you were 3. he were	1. we were 2. you were 3. they were
Present Perfect Tense	1. I have been 2. you have been 3. he have been	1. we have been 2. you have been 3. they have been
Past Perfect Tense	1. I had been 2. you had been 3. he had been	1. we had been 2. you had been 3. they had been

IMPERATIVE MOOD		
Present Tense	be	be

	Present	**Past**	**Perfect**
Infinitives	to be		to have been
Participles	being	been	having been
Gerunds	being		having been

207   CONJUGATION OF THE VERB *SEE*

Active Voice

INDICATIVE MOOD		Singular	Plural
Present Tense		1. I see	1. we see
		2. you see	2. you see
		3. he sees	3. they see
Past Tense		1. I saw	1. we saw
		2. you saw	2. you saw
		3. he saw	3. they saw
Future Tense		1. I shall see	1. we shall see
		2. you will see	2. you will see
		3. he will see	3. they will see
Present Perfect Tense		1. I have seen	1. we have seen
		2. you have seen	2. you have seen
		3. he has seen	3. they have seen
Past Perfect Tense		1. I had seen	1. we had seen
		2. you had seen	2. you had seen
		3. he had seen	3. they had seen
Future Perfect Tense		1. I shall have seen	1. we shall have seen
		2. you will have seen	2. you will have seen
		3. he will have seen	3. they will have seen

SUBJUNCTIVE MOOD			
Present Tense		1. I see	1. we see
		2. you see	2. you see
		3. he see	3. they see
Past Tense		1. I saw	1. we saw
		2. you saw	2. you saw
		3. he saw	3. they saw
Present Perfect Tense		1. I have seen	1. we have seen
		2. you have seen	2. you have seen
		3. he have seen	3. they have seen
Past Perfect Tense		1. I had seen	1. we had seen
		2. you had seen	2. you had seen
		3. he had seen	3. they had seen

IMPERATIVE MOOD			
Present Tense		see	see

	Present	**Past**	**Perfect**
Infinitives	to see		to have seen
Participles	seeing	seen	having seen
Gerunds	seeing		having seen

208   CONJUGATION OF THE VERB *SEE*

Passive Voice

INDICATIVE MOOD | **Singular** | **Plural**

Present Tense
1. I am seen
2. you are seen
3. he is seen

1. we are seen
2. you are seen
3. they are seen

Past Tense
1. I was seen
2. you were seen
3. he was seen

1. we were seen
2. you were seen
3. they were seen

Future Tense
1. I shall be seen
2. you will be seen
3. he will be seen

1. we shall be seen
2. you will be seen
3. they will be seen

Present Perfect Tense
1. I have been seen
2. you have been seen
3. he has been seen

1. we have been seen
2. you have been seen
3. they have been seen

Past Perfect Tense
1. I had been seen
2. you had been seen
3. he had been seen

1. we had been seen
2. you had been seen
3. they had been seen

Future Perfect Tense
1. I shall have been seen
2. you will have been seen
3. he will have been seen

1. we shall have been seen
2. you will have been seen
3. they will have been seen

SUBJUNCTIVE MOOD

Present Tense
1. I be seen
2. you be seen
3. he be seen

1. we be seen
2. you be seen
3. they be seen

Past Tense
1. I were seen
2. you were seen
3. he were seen

1. we were seen
2. you were seen
3. they were seen

Present Perfect Tense
1. I have been seen
2. you have been seen
3. he have been seen

1. we have been seen
2. you have been seen
3. they have been seen

Past Perfect Tense
1. I had been seen
2. you had been seen
3. he had been seen

1. we had been seen
2. you had been seen
3. they had been seen

IMPERATIVE MOOD

Present Tense   be seen   be seen

	Present	**Past**	**Perfect**
Infinitives	to be seen		to have been seen
Participles	being seen	seen	having been seen
Gerunds	being seen		having been seen

209   CONJUGATION OF THE VERB *SEE* – PROGRESSIVE FORM

Active Voice

INDICATIVE MOOD		**Singular**	**Plural**
Present Tense		1. I am seeing	1. we are seeing
		2. you are seeing	2. you are seeing
		3. he is seeing	3. they are seeing
Past Tense		1. I was seeing	1. we were seeing
		2. you were seeing	2. you were seeing
		3. he was seeing	3. they were seeing
Future Tense		1. I shall be seeing	1. we shall be seeing
		2. you will be seeing	2. you will be seeing
		3. he will be seeing	3. they will be seeing
Present Perfect Tense		1. I have been seeing	1. we have been seeing
		2. you have been seeing	2. you have been seeing
		3. he has been seeing	3. they have been seeing
Past Perfect Tense		1. I had been seeing	1. we had been seeing
		2. you had been seeing	2. you had been seeing
		3. he had been seeing	3. they had been seeing
Future Perfect Tense		1. I shall have been seeing	1. we shall have been seeing
		2. you will have been seeing	2. you will have been seeing
		3. he will have been seeing	3. they will have been seeing

SUBJUNCTIVE MOOD			
Present Tense		1. I be seeing	1. we be seeing
		2. you be seeing	2. you be seeing
		3. he be seeing	3. they be seeing
Past Tense		1. I were seeing	1. we were seeing
		2. you were seeing	2. you were seeing
		3. he were seeing	3. they were seeing

	Present	**Perfect**
Infinitives	to be seeing	to have been seeing
Participles		having been seeing

210   CONJUGATION OF THE VERB *SEE* – PROGRESSIVE FORM

Passive Voice

INDICATIVE MOOD		**Singular**	**Plural**
Present Tense		1. I am being seen	1. we are being seen
		2. you are being seen	2. you are being seen
		3. he is being seen	3. they are being seen
Past Tense		1. I was being seen	1. we were being seen
		2. you were being seen	2. you were being seen
		3. he was being seen	3. they were being seen

211   Besides the tense forms given in 206, 207, 208, two other forms are frequently used: the **progressive** (209, 210) and the **emphatic**.

212   The **progressive form** represents action as continuing at the time noted. This
form is also called the **present (past, future, etc.) continuous** by many grammarians. It is made by placing some form of the verb *to be* before the present
participle (201):

    I *am seeing*—you *are seeing*—he *is seeing*.

    Although the present-participle form is used in making the progressive verb
phrase, the participle is here considered not as a participle but as a part of
the entire verb phrase:

    David *is painting* a picture. (*Painting*, though present participle in form, is
here considered to be a part of the verb phrase *is painting*.)

213   The **emphatic form** gives emphasis to the present or past form of the verb in
the active voice (184) by the use of *do, does,* or *did*. Forms of *do* are used
also in negative statements and in questions without emphasis:

    I *do see.*   She *does see.*   He *did see.* (**emphatic**)
    Do you see?   I *do* not see. (**not emphatic**)

214   The **synopsis** of a verb is the correct arrangement of its moods (187–189);
voices (184–185), and tenses (191–196) in **one person** (69) and **number** (73);
it is an abbreviated conjugation (205).

215   SYNOPSIS OF THE VERB *SEE*

    in the Third Person, Singular Number

INDICATIVE MOOD	Active	Passive
Present Tense	he sees	he is seen
Past Tense	he saw	he was seen
Future Tense	he will see	he will be seen
Present Perfect Tense	he has seen	he has been seen
Past Perfect Tense	he had seen	he had been seen
Future Perfect Tense	he will have seen	he will have been seen

SUBJUNCTIVE MOOD		
Present Tense	he see	he be seen
Past Tense	he saw	he were seen
Present Perfect Tense	he have seen	he have been seen
Past Perfect Tense	he had seen	he had been seen

(The imperative mood is used in the second person only.)

Exercise 2.17   Using Verbs.
    Copy the following sentences, crossing out each incorrect verb form and writ-
ing the correction above it.

                            done   *saw*
    EXAMPLE: He has ~~did~~ that since we ~~seen~~ him.

a. He taken the chair and drug it to the table.
b. It gives us a thrill to see how fast the team had ran.
c. The glass from which he had drank was broke.
d. She had rode for hours and had not ate.
e. Bob has chose his topic but has not yet began writing his report.
f. Jack come to the meeting, but he has now went back to his class again.
g. We had sang all the songs that we knowed.
h. If you had went with us, you would have saw a good picture.
i. He would have went over the side of the pool if we had not drug him back.
j. No one drunk or eat enough at supper to please the hosts.
k. He had took a look at what she had wrote.
l. You had not yet came when Bob give his talk.
m. He has drove faster than we have ran.
n. One of the poems that she had wrote was chose for the program.
o. They had began the return journey early in the morning and had drove until dark.
p. She begun to praise him for the part that he had took in the play.
q. We haven't saw Jane since we eat dinner.
r. He has just sang some songs that were wrote by Hal David and Burt Bachrach.
s. She should have gave us the plans before we done the work.
t. Because the horse had not been broke, no one had yet rode him.
u. This might have been did differently if she had came with us.

Usage

216   Five frequently used verbs that cause much trouble are the following: *come, go, do, see, give.*

> Bob *came* (not *come*) yesterday.
> He had *come* (not *came*) when I left.
> She had *gone* (not *went*) when you came.
> May *did* (not *done*) the work well.
> She has *done* (not *did*) good work.
> I *saw* (not *seen*) her yesterday.
> Tom had *seen* (not *saw*) the show.
> Ann *gave* (not *give*) me this book.
> Pat had *given* (not *gave*) her a camera.

217   These three pairs of verbs are often confused: *lie–lay, sit–set, rise–raise.*

Lie, sit, and *rise* are always intransitive (175) in their usual meanings. *Lay, set,* and *raise* are usually transitive (174) and, therefore, must have an object to complete the meaning:

> Let us *lie* here and rest.   I *laid* the book there yesterday.

She *sits* by the window to read.   I *set* the box on the shelf.
The cake did not *rise* well.   Did you *raise* the flag?

218 The verbs *lay* and *set* may be used as intransitives in certain of their second-ary meanings:

The hen *lays* well.
The sun *set* at six o'clock yesterday.
This jelly did not *set* well.
We eagerly *set* out on our long journey.

Exercise 2.18   Forming Tenses.

A verb is given at the beginning of each group of sentences below. For each sentence write the tense form of this verb called for in the parentheses. The **p** following the tense indication means that the form is to be passive; otherwise all forms are to be active.

EXAMPLES: **break**

(past perfect) The wind ___*had broken*___ three windows.

(present perfect–p) Three windows ___*have been broken*___ by the wind.

give

a. (past) Are you sure that he_____you the correct number of tickets?
b. (future) Larry_____ you your tickets by noon tomorrow.
c. (past–p) The prize _____ to the person who sold the most tickets?
d. (present perfect) Pat's mother_____us an order for 30 tickets.

come

e. (future perfect) They_____to the meeting by seven.
f. (past) The boys _____early to help clean up the clubroom.
g. (present perfect) Some girls_____to help us set up the chairs.

lie

h. (present) Our big black cat often_____on that window seat.
i. (past perfect) One day we found that he_____on the mantel all night.
j. (past) We _____ on the lawn and watched him try to catch a blowing leaf.
k. (present perfect) That lazy cat_____there and watched us all day.

raise

l. (past) The chairperson quickly _____the question himself.
m. (past perfect–p) A discussion _____ about the last motion.

rise

n. (past perfect) Ken_____from treasurer to chairperson in a short time.
o. (past) The students _____to their feet when the president entered.
p. (present perfect) The chairperson_____to introduce the speaker.

sit

q. (present) That old man＿＿＿ alone in the park every day.

r. (past perfect) He＿＿＿ there often before we ever noticed him.

s. (past) We＿＿＿ in the boat while Jim rowed it around the pond.

t. (present perfect—p) The bench＿＿＿on by many different people.

219 *May* is used to express permission; *can* refers to ability:

    May I go to town?   *Can* the bird fly?

Some writers use *can* for permission, but this usage is still considered too colloquial or informal for written use.

220 The following rules governing the use of *shall* and *will, should* and *would* (221-24), are seldom stressed because of a wide variation in actual practice that makes them largely interchangeable.

221 In formal writing use *shall* in the first person and *will* in the second and third persons for the simple future tense:

    I *shall* sing this afternoon.
    You *will* succeed.
    He *will* stay at home.

222 To express determination, desire, or a promise, reverse the normal order and use *will* in the first person and *shall* in the second and third persons:

    I *will* be there.
    You *shall* not go.
    They *shall* be brought to justice.

223 Use *shall* in all persons in object (noun) clauses after verbs of *deciding, wishing, demanding, willing,* etc.:

    He insists that they *shall* not follow him.

224 The uses of *should* and *would* correspond to those of *shall* and *will:*

    1. For simple future, use *should* with the first person, and use *would* with the second and third.
    2. For determination, reverse the order.

225 *Had ought to* is never correct as a combination for *ought to* or *should:*

    He *should* (or *ought to,* not *had ought to*) work.

226 The use of the word *loan* as a verb is interchangeable with *lend* in matters of money but is more restricted in other meanings:

    He *loaned* me ten dollars.   He *lent* his bicycle.

227 Do not confuse *leave* and *let, learn* and *teach.* To *leave* means to go *away from;* to *let* means to *permit* or to *allow:*

    She will *let* (not *leave*) us use her pen.

To learn means *to get information; to teach* means *to give information:*

He will *teach* (not *learn*) me to paint.

228 *Accept* and *except* are often confused. *To accept* means *to take; to except* means *to leave out* or *to exclude:*

I *accept* the gift.
If we *except* her picture from the show, she will feel hurt.

229 Although *ain't* is usually condemned as nonstandard, we need some good word to take its place:

The roses *aren't* (not *ain't*) in bloom yet.
I am to blame, *am I not* (not *ain't*)?

In England, the form *aren't I* is considered correct in the preceding sentence. Although this form has gained favor in this country, some American authorities still classify it as informal.

230 Never use *of* as a substitute for *have:*

She should *have* (not *of*) gone home.

231 Avoid using *and* for *to* with the verb *try:*

Questionable: Try *and* help him.
Correct: Try *to* help him.

232 After certain words the *to* is generally omitted from the infinitive (199). Some of these words are *bid, dare, let, make, help, need, see:*

Let us (without *to*) go to the show.

233 There is some objection to the use of *but what* for *but that* after negative forms of verbs:

Questionable: He did not know *but what* I left.
Informal: He did not know *but that* I left.
Formal: He did not know *that* I left.

234 Do not use *help but* in the sense of *avoid* in formal writing:

Colloquial: He could not *help but* laugh.
Formal: He could not *help* laughing.

235 The **split infinitive**—the use of a word between the parts of an infinitive (199)— is not at all incorrect, but it usually makes an awkward sentence unless carefully controlled:

Awkward: She told me *to not help* him.
Better: She told me *not to help* him.

Exercise 2.19   Verb Usage.
Copy each of the following sentences, crossing out the incorrect verb forms

and writing the correction just above it.

ought   teach

EXAMPLE: You ~~had ought~~ to let me ~~learn~~ you.

- a. You done well, but you could of done much better.
- b. I had knowed that he would not leave the child fall from the swing.
- c. He set up before he begun to write.
- d. I knowed that I had gave you the movies that were took at the picnic.
- e. As I raised up in bed, I seen him.
- f. The scarf that is laying on the table was give to me by my grandmother.
- g. The papers were laying there on the desk when I last seen them.
- h. The desk lamp that my aunt give me for Christmas was broke when it come.
- i. Why don't Justine leave you learn her to knit?
- j. Real all the directions before you try and answer the questions.
- k. He could have ran faster if he had chose to wear his other shoes.
- l. You had ought to have spoken more distinctly when you give your report.
- m. Haven't the officers did anything to find the money that was took?
- n. Janet, as well as her friends, were nearly froze by the walk in the wind.
- o. After we had drank the lemonade, we set down in the shade.
- p. He hadn't drove very far when it begun to snow very hard.
- q. The boys must of went as soon as the bell had rang.
- r. Had she knowed who had broke the dish?
- s. Can I show you the cartoon I drawed?
- t. You should of spoke to the coach before the game.

Agreement of Verb and Subject

236 A verb should agree with its subject in person and number (69-75, 197).

237 Words that are joined to a subject by *with, accompanied by, together with, as well as, no less than,* or *including* do not change the number of the subject:

> The teacher, as well as the students, *was* there.
> The students, as well as the teacher, *were* there.

238 Two or more singular subjects joined by *or* or *nor* require a singular verb:

> Neither Esther nor Ruth *was* present.

♦ When a subject is composed of both singular and plural forms joined by *or* or *nor,* the verb must agree with the nearer subject:

> Two other boys or Henry *is* to   Neither he nor the boys *play*
> blame!   golf.

239 In a sentence beginning with *here* or *there*, the number of the verb is determined by the number of the substantive following it:

There *is* a book on the table.   There *are* hats in the window.
Here *are* Bob and Sue.   There *go* Joe and Fred.

♦ When *there* is used as an introductory word, as in the first two sentences, it is called an **expletive**. An expletive is a word which, without special meaning of its own, introduces a subject or object that follows. *It* is another word frequently used in this way:

It is good to be here.   Make *it* clear that she is invited.

240   A collective noun (59) takes a singular verb when the group is considered as a unit and takes a plural verb when the individuals are considered (92):

Our football team *is* popular.   The team *have* received their
                                          sweaters.

241   In expressions such as *one of the girls who, one of the trees which,* and *one of the persons that,* the verb in the relative clause agrees with the antecedent of the relative pronoun (135):

He is one of those teachers who *are* inspiring. (The antecedent of *who* is teachers.)
She is the only one of the group that *understands.* (The antecedent of *that* is *one.*)

242   *Each, either, neither, someone, somebody, anyone, anybody, everyone, everybody, no one, nobody, one,* and *a person* are singular (163, 164):

Each of the students *was* (not *were*) questioned.
Neither Rosa nor Tim *was* (not *were*) home.

243   If *plenty, abundance,* or *rest* is modified by a phrase introduced by *of,* the verb agrees with the noun in the phrase:

Plenty of potatoes *are* grown in Colorado.
An abundance of meat *was* provided.

♦ Fractions are used in this same way:

One third of the paper *was* sold.   One fifth of the boats *were* lost.

244   If the word *number* is preceded by *a* and followed by *of,* it takes a plural verb; if it is preceded by *the,* it requires a singular verb:

A number of men *were* hurt.   The number of accidents *is* great.

245   A noun that refers to an amount of money, a space of time, or a unit of measurement is singular in meaning even though the form is plural:

Fifty cents *is* the price.   Ten miles *is* a long way to walk.

246 Except as noted in 241, a phrase (389) between the subject and the verb does not affect the verb:

One of the girls *is* my friend.

247 If the subject of the verb is made up of two or more words joined by *and,* the verb is plural:

Helen and Grace *are* here.

♦ If the two are thought of as a unit, the verb is singular:

Bread and butter *is* a good food.

♦ In asking questions beginning with verbs, it is necessary to be careful:

Are Grace and her sister here?

248 If a subject consists of two or more nouns, only one of which is expressed, the verb is plural:

A red and a blue book *are* on the desk.

249 A verb introduced by a relative pronoun (135) has the same number and person as the noun or pronoun to which it refers:

He gave the book to me who *am* (not *is*) its owner.

Exercise 2.20   Verb Agreement.
Furnish the correct forms of the verbs given at the beginning of each group.

Part 1. is—are

a. Ruth, with her two cousins, _____ coming for a visit.
b. Either Fred or Don _____ the captain.
c. Each of the players _____ making good grades.
d. Both candidates for the office _____ qualified.
e. One of her relatives _____ a millionaire.
f. _____ Ramon or Lola going with us?
g. Neither the coach nor the players _____ pleased with the new suits.

Part 2. has—have

h. Several rooms in the house _____ been redecorated.
i. Neither the twins nor their sister _____ missed any school this year.
j. _____ either of the reports been given?
k. Each of the members _____ been assigned a different task.
l. _____ one of the students arranged the flowers for the reception?

Part 3. was—were

m. The house, with all of its furnishings, _____ destroyed by fire.
n. The teachers, as well as the new principal, _____ invited.
o. Every one of the dresses _____ small.

p. Neither the teachers nor the principal _____ happy about it.
q. The players on the second team _____ sitting on the bench.
r. The Board of Education_____ meeting in its new library.
s. The choir_____ marching onto the stage in their new dark red robes.

Part 4. doesn't—don't

t. Hank says that he _____ want to go.
u. _____ the seniors know better than that?
v. _____ one of you know him?

Exercise 2.21   Reviewing Verb Agreement.
Copy only those sentences that contain incorrect verb forms, crossing out each error and writing the correct form above it.

were
EXAMPLE: There ~~was~~ twelve girls in the group, but only four were sophomores. (239)

a. Kay doesn't know that a number of her friends has been invited. (197, 244)
b. It seems that Bob don't know which of the girls is leader. (197, 246)
c. Doesn't the hat and jacket lying on that chair belong to Rolando? (197)
d. A large number of students is going to the table tennis match today. (244)
e. We thought that twenty dollars were too much for that old chair. (245)
f. The number of traffic accidents over Memorial Day was very large. (244)
g. One of the boys are here, but neither of the girls has come yet. (246, 245)
h. Helen is one of those people who is always very competitive. (197, 241)
i. Everyone of the girls now speak more confidently. (242)
j. Jenny, as well as Sue, were here; but there were others to come. (237, 239)
k. A black and a blue car was parked in front of Jim's house yesterday. (248)
l. Ask one of those clerks who are always so pleasant. (241)
m. There is two volunteers to work at the booth, but one of them is not here. (239, 246)
n. Each of the columnists think that our team is sure to win the soccer trophy. (242, 240)
o. There are many good desserts, but peaches and cream are my favorite. (239, 247)
p. Neither Kay nor Dan have joined the club, but Jean and Lou are members. (238, 247)
q. Neither the typists nor the secretary have been here since last semester. (238)
r. Neither Ed nor the newcomers has sent the money to the treasurer. (238, 247)
s. The jury have made a decision, and everyone is eager to hear the verdict. (240, 242)

t. Neither Hank nor Nina thinks that fifty dollars is too much for that old car. (237, 245)

Sequence of Tenses

250 If the verb in the main clause (397) is in the past tense (193), the verb in the dependent clause (398) may be in the past tense:

Jennifer said that she *expected* to go home.

251 The past tense in the main clause (397) may be followed by the present tense in the dependent clause (398) when it expresses a general truth:

Columbus believed that the earth *is* round.

252 An idea once established as truth, now known to be untrue, is expressed in the past tense:

The ancients believed that the earth *was* flat.

253 SEQUENCE OF TENSES IN INDIRECT DISCOURSE (Reported Speech)

a. Present or "now" time, or possible future time
b. Intended or completed action in past time
c. Intended or completed action in future time

1. **Present**
    Ben *says* that a. he *is going* (*goes*) with us.
                    b. he *was going* (*went*) with us.
                    c. he *will be going* (*will go*) with us.

2. **Past**
    Ben *said* that a. he *is going* (*goes*) with us.
                   b. he *was going* (*went*) with us.
                   c. he *will be going* (*will go*) with us.

3. **Future**
    Ben *will say* that a. he *is going* (*goes*) with us.
                       b. he *was going* (*went*) with us.
                       c. he *will be going* (*will go*) with us.

4. **Present Perfect**
    Ben *has said* that a. he *is going* (*goes*) with us.
                       b. he *was going* (*went*) with us.
                       c. he *would be going* (*would go*) with us.

5. **Past Perfect**
    Ben *had said* that a. he *is going* (*goes*) with us.
                       b. he *was going* (*went*) with us.
                       b. he *had been going* (*had gone*) with us.
                       c. he *would have been going* (*would have gone*) with us.

6. **Future Perfect**

Ben *will have said* that 　a. 　he *is going* (*goes*) with us.

　　　　　　　　　　　　b. 　he *was going* (*went*) with us.

　　　　　　　　　　　　b. 　he *had been going* (*had gone*) with us.

　　　　　　　　　　　　c. 　he *would have been going* (*would have gone*) with us.

This chart shows all the possible relationships. Numbers 1, 2, 4, and 5 are used in statement-of-fact situations; numbers 3 and 6 reflect a qualifying or conditional statement which suggests that a clause, such as "if he were asked," has not been expressed though it is implied.

Special Uses of Voice, Tense, and Number

254 　Do not shift illogically from the active voice (184) to the passive (185) in the same sentence.

As we came over the hill, we *saw a deer* (not a *deer was seen*).

255 　Use the active voice (184) unless there is some self-evident reason for using the passive:

We *heard a noise* (not A *noise was heard*).

256 　In expressing a **wish or a condition contrary to fact**, use *were*, not *was*:

If I *were* he, I'd go home. 　　　　　I wish she *were* the governor.

257 　In a past **condition not contrary to fact**, the indicative mood (187) is used, not the subjunctive (189) as in 256:

If John *was* present, I did not see him.

258 　After *as if* and *as though*, use the subjunctive *were*:

She speaks as though she *were* angry.

259 　With words expressing **command** or **necessity**, use either the present subjunctive form (189) or a verb-phrase:

It is necessary that the boy *be* (or *should be*) dismissed immediately.
It was necessary that he *be* dismissed.

260 　Use *are* or *were* with you, even when the pronoun is singular:

Edgar, you *were* there. 　　　　　*Are* you there, now?

261 　When one subject is affirmative and the other negative, the verb agrees with the affirmative:

Your honesty, not your pleas, *causes* me to relent.

262 　In the use of **arithmetical expressions** there has been disagreement as to the

correct verb forms, but the following are accepted:

Six divided by three *is* two.	Seven minus two *is* five.
One fourth of twelve *is* three.	Five plus three *is* eight.
Five times two *are* ten.	Three and four *are* seven.

263 When the **infinitive** (199) refers to a time coincident with that of the main verb or some time after it, use the present infinitive:

I intended *to sing* (not *to have sung*).

The **present infinitive** (199, 206) may be used with a main verb in any tense, as follows:

She wishes *to meet* you.	She had wished *to meet* you.
She wished *to meet* you.	She will wish *to meet* you.
She has wished *to meet* you.	She will have wished *to meet* you.

When the **perfect infinitive** (199, 206) is used with a verb in the past tense or in the past perfect tense (193, 194) expressing *desire, hope,* or *duty,* it indicates that something interfered with the desire, hope, or duty:

She wished *to have seen* you. (She did not see you.)
I hoped *to have met* you. (I did not meet you.)

When the present infinitive is used after one of these verbs there is an element of uncertainty:

He hoped *to meet* you. (Whether he did or not is uncertain.)

The use of the perfect infinitive (199, 206) after such verbs as *seem, appear,* and *know* shows that the event denoted by the infinitive took place before the time indicated by the verb:

Bob seems *to have succeeded.*

264 It is incorrect to use a present participle when indicating an action previous to that expressed by the main verb:

He has been away three days, *having left* (not *leaving*) last Monday.

Uses of the Verbals

265 The **infinitive** (199, 232) has many uses:

    a. The infinitive used as a noun (56, 61*e*, 393):.
        1. **Subject of a verb** (95): *To win* is not easy.
        2. **Predicate nominative** (96): What she wants is *to win.*
        3. **Object of a verb** (102): He likes *to write.*
        4. **Nominative case in apposition with the subject** (100): His aim, *to succeed,* is commendable.
        5. **Objective case in apposition with object** (111): She has one great desire, *to succeed.*

b. The infinitive used as an **adjective** (277): The house *to be sold* is new.

c. The infinitive used as an **adverb** (316): Mary came *to see* us.

DIAGRAM—An infinitive used as subject:

To succeed is his intention.

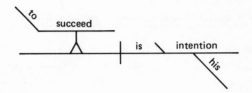

266 The **gerund** (56, 61*d*, 200) has many noun uses, as follows:

a. **Subject of a verb:** *Stealing* is wrong.

b. **Object of verb:** I heard the *roaring* of the river.

c. **Object of preposition:** Were they punished for *cheating?*

d. **Apposition:** His work, *mining,* was dangerous.

e. **Predicate nominative:** Her work is *painting* signs.

DIAGRAM—A gerund used as **subject** (266*a*) and having an object:

Running races is good exercise.

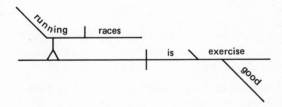

DIAGRAM—A gerund used as **object** (266*b*) and having an object:

The boys dislike *picking* cotton.

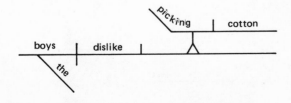

267 Most authorities agree that a verbal may be considered a pure noun when it has lost the verbal idea; when it may be pluralized; when it may be preceded by an article and followed by a preposition; or when it is the name of an art, a course of study, or some form of activity:

We attended the *wedding*.	The *rowing* of the boat was easy.
I know Bob's *drawings*.	I am taking a course in *writing*.

268 A **compound gerund** is formed by placing a noun before a gerund: *mountain climbing, skin diving.*

The gerund is also called **verbal noun** or **participial noun** (200).

♦ There are some grammarians who believe there is a difference between the gerund and the verbal noun, but the difference is one of identification rather than of use and function.

269 The **participle** is a verbal (198, 201) which is used as an adjective. It has the same uses as the regular adjective (275):

    a. **Attributive** (276):
        The *running* stream is beautiful.   A *broken* limb of the tree has fallen.
    b. **Predicate adjective** (179, 278, 289):
        The game was *thrilling*.   The boy is *discouraged*.
    c. **Appositive adjective** (277):
        The girl, *running* swiftly, soon disappeared.
        The limb, *broken* by the wind, has fallen down.

The participle ending in *ing* sometimes seems to be a pure adjective, and at other times it is thought of as a part of the verb-phrase in the progressive form (212):

The *gleaming* stars are beautiful. (resembles a pure **adjective)**
The stars, *gleaming* in the sky, are beautiful. (**regular participle)**
The stars are *gleaming* in the sky. (**part of the verb)**

The past participle (201) is sometimes used as an adjective and sometimes as the main part of the verb in the passive voice (185):

This drama, *written* by Thornton Wilder, is my favorite. (**adjective)**
This book *was written* by Rachel Carson. (**part of the passive verb form)**

DIAGRAM—A participle (201) having an object:

John, *fearing defeat*, encouraged his comrades.

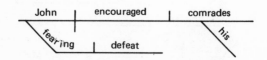

270 A noun or pronoun introducing a gerund is usually in the possessive case (116, 127):

He approved *Ann's* (not *Ann*) selling the book.

He did not like *my* (not *me*) going away.

This rule is not rigidly observed in conversation and informal writing.

♦ It will sometimes require close observation to distinguish the participle from the gerund:

We referred to the girl *playing* tennis. (**participle**)
We referred to the girl's *playing* tennis. (**gerund**)

271   A **participial phrase** (390*c*) or a **prepositional gerund phrase** should have a substantive (47) that it can logically modify expressed in the sentence. When the substantive is omitted, the modifying phrase is said to be **dangling**. Dangling modifiers often result in absurdities. Be sure to give modifiers something to modify (451):

Running to the window, I saw a fire (not a *fire was seen*).   (390*c*) (The participial phrase *running to the window* modifies *I*. The fire was not running to the window.)
By working hard, we finished the task (not the *task was finished*).   (390*d*) (The prepositional phrase *by working hard,* which has a gerund as the object of the preposition, modifies *we*.)
Sitting in the moonlight, we enjoyed the music (not the *music was enjoyed*).

♦ A few set phrases, such as *generally speaking, considering everything,* are understood to modify the entire sentence, not any particular substantive in it; they are then called **sentence modifiers**.

272   **Punctuation** of participles and gerunds is very important. Note the use of the comma (499) in the examples just given. If a participial phrase begins the sentence, it is followed by a comma:

Running quickly, the girl won the race.

The absolute construction (99) is set off from the rest of the sentence by a comma or commas:

The game being ended, we went home.

Sometimes the word *being* is omitted from the absolute construction, but the comma is used:

The matter (being) *adjusted,* we felt relieved.

♦ Nonrestrictive phrases (phrases not necessary to the meaning of the rest of the sentence) are set off by commas (499):

The man *sitting by the desk* is the principal. (**necessary**—no commas used)
The old man, *sitting idly in the sun,* dreamed of other days. (**unnecessary**—commas used)

273   The **subject of an infinitive** (108, 199) is in the objective case:

We asked *him* to go. (*Him* is the subject of *to go*.)
Jack asked *her* to sing. (*Her* is the subject of *to sing*.)

♦ In an **infinitive clause** (401) a predicate noun (96) or a predicate pronoun (145*b*) used after *to be* is in the objective case to agree with the subject of the infinitive (109):

You thought us to be *them*.
They took me to be *her*.

274   If the infinitive *to be* has no subject, the predicate noun or the predicate pronoun following it is in the nominative case (109):

He was thought to be *I*.
I was believed to be *she*.

Exercise 2.22   Using and Punctuating Verbals.

Part I.   Determine which form in boldface shows the more acceptable use of verbals in the following sentences.

EXAMPLE: <u>1</u> Walking in the rain, [1]**we needed boots**/[2]**boots were needed.**

a. Hurrying down the path, [1]**the garden was soon reached**/[2]**he soon reached the garden.**
b. After working all day, [1]**the job was completed**/[2]**we completed the job.**
c. Bill told us about [1]**Ann**/[2]**Ann's** leaving.
d. Evelyn makes an effort [1]**not to**/[2]**to not** make errors in speech.
e. Dad objected to [1]**me**/[2] **my** whistling.
f. Hiking in the woods, [1]**many flowers were found**/[2]**we found many flowers.**
g. The chairperson was not in favor of [1]**their**/[2]**them** making the report.
h. Going to the door, [1]**a strange sight was seen**/[2]**I saw a strange sight.**
i. Wandering along the path, [1]**we saw a fountain**/[2]**a fountain was seen.**
j. Elva did not like [1]**you**/[2]**your** refusing to sing.
k. He aimed [1]**to not**/[2]**not to** go early.
l. By refusing the gift, [1]**my friend was offended**/[2]**I offended my friend.**

Part II.   Some of the following sentences contain introductory phrases and nonrestrictive phrases that require punctuation. Copy the sentences, inserting commas where necessary.

a. The teacher coming into the classroom found Dan sitting there.
b. Giving the report alone Hal had difficulty.
c. The boy giving the lesson is my brother.
d. Kay and Jim having stopped to shop were late.
e. Marko wearing a dark suit left for church.
f. The girl eating the sandwich came forward.
g. Seeing the coach Paul congratulated him.
h. Expecting company Mother stayed at home.

i. Peggy having worked all summer at last had money for a new oboe.
j. Sizing up the pool he took a shallow dive.
k. Estimating construction costs was her job.
l. Pleasing no one he chose the colors himself.
m. The car belching smoke finally started.

ADJECTIVES

275 An **adjective** is a modifier (7) which describes or limits a substantive (47). It may be a word or a group of words (7, 8, 9, 42):

We saw *beautiful* flowers.

Those flowers *on the desk* are roses. (*Those* is a simple modifier; the group is a phrase modifier, 390*a*.)

Those boys *whom you saw* are students. (*Those* is a simple modifier; the group is a clause modifier, 408.)

The adjective is used effectively in painting word pictures—describing (563). Note the effect of the added modifiers (7) in the illustrations below:

Near the house stood a tree. (**unimpressive**)

Above the old-fashioned, stone dwelling a slender eucalyptus tree waved its feathery branches in the morning sunlight. (**vivid**)

Adjectives are used in three ways: **attributive, appositive,** and **predicate.**

276 The **attributive** use of the adjective is that of the direct modifier that precedes the substantive:

The man wore a *dark* suit.

♦ Adjectives in a series are separated by commas (505):

A *beautiful, tall, slender* pine stood nearby.

277 The **appositive** use of the adjective directly follows the substantive that it modifies:

The speaker, *tall* and *graceful,* soon won the audience. (The adjectives *tall* and *graceful* explain the appearance of the speaker. The adjective used appositively is set off by a comma or commas.)

278 The **predicate** use of the adjective (179-180) is to complete the meaning of the predicate and modify the subject:

The work was *difficult.*   Mountains are *beautiful.*

♦ The predicate adjective is usually joined to the subject by a linking verb (179), such as *be* and *become,* or by such verbs of the senses as *seems, appears, looks, tastes, feels, smells, sounds;* also *remains, turns, grows, stays, continues.*

♦ Predicate adjectives (and predicate nominatives, 96) may also occur after certain verbs (104) in the passive voice (185):

She was considered *intelligent.*

279   An adjective that describes a substantive (47) by expressing some quality belonging to it is called a **descriptive adjective**:

We saw *tall* trees.   They climbed *high* hills.

280   An adjective that describes a substantive or that limits its meaning without expressing a quality is called a **limiting** or **definitive adjective**:

She sent us *those* books.   We saw *many* trees.

281   The limiting or definitive adjectives include **pronouns used as adjectives** (pronominal adjectives, both indefinite and demonstrative, 138, 139, 140), **numeral adjectives,** and the **articles**.

Pronouns in the possessive case (116, 117) are sometimes called **possessive adjectives** (131, 146):

John lost *his* book.

The **pronominal adjectives** (140) are given under the treatment of pronouns (131, 138, 139), but further illustrations of their uses are given here. Be sure to distinguish between the pronoun use and the adjective use:

This book is a grammar. **(adjective)**
This is a book. **(pronoun,** 138)
Each should bring a book. **(pronoun)**
Each student should bring a book. **(adjective)**
We saw *her* at the movies. **(pronoun in the objective case)**
We saw *her* book on the desk. **(pronoun in the possessive case:** also called a **possessive adjective,** 131)

282   **Numeral adjectives** indicate number. There are two classes which are generally used: **cardinal** and **ordinal**.

283   The **cardinal** number indicates how many items there are in a group or set:

We saw *three* ships.

284   The **ordinal** number gives the order of the items in a sequence:

He won the *third* prize.

285   The adjectives *a, an,* and *the* are called **articles**.

286   *A* and *an* are called **indefinite articles** because they do not point out particular persons, places, or things—*a* and *an* are modified forms of *one:*

The camper saw a deer and *an* eagle. (*An* is used before a word beginning with one of the vowel sounds—*a, e, i, o, u.* Before a consonant sound, *a* is used.)

287 *The* is called the **definite article** because it points out a particular member of a class of persons, places, or things—*the* is a modified form of *that*.

This is *the* book we need.

♦ *The* may also be used to indicate a generalized noun as a representative of its class:

We have now studied *the* noun, *the* verb, and *the* adjective.

288 The **proper adjective** is derived from a proper noun (55) or is a proper noun used as an adjective and is written with a capital letter.

Although he is a *Chinese* student, he enjoys the *Colorado* climate.

289 Avoid substituting an adverb (316) for an adjective after a linking verb (179):

The rose smells *sweet* (not *sweetly*).
He looks *bad* (not *badly*) since his illness.

290 Many words commonly used as **pronouns** may be used as modifying **adjectives** (138, 139, 281):

That hat is made of fur.   I know *what* man you mean.
Which horse is yours?   *Any* boy can do *that* work.

♦ When the noun that is modified is omitted, each of the adjectives of this class becomes a pronoun (138, 139, 281):

That is made of fur. **(pronoun)**

Exercise 2.23   Recognizing Adjectives

Copy the following sentences, drawing one line under each adjective and a second line under each predicate adjective. Do not underline any adjective used as part of a proper noun.

EXAMPLE: Several national parks are very large.

a. Each national park in the country was established to preserve some outstanding natural wonder, a scenic or historic area.
b. Yellowstone Park in Wyoming is the largest, oldest, and best-known park.
c. Here famous geysers, hot springs, and mud volcanoes attract much attention.
d. Old Faithful, the popular, world-famous geyser, erupts on the hour.
e. Not far away to the south rise the towering peaks of the Grand Tetons.
f. The Grand Canyon of the Yellowstone River in Arizona is a colorful and inspiring sight, unmatched anywhere else in the world.
g. Glacier Park in Montana has sixty glaciers and numerous beautiful lakes.
h. This is an area of gigantic snow-covered peaks, rushing streams, and picturesque valleys.
i. One of the great spectacles of this park is the colorful display of native wildflowers.

j. Crater Lake in Oregon is the deepest lake in North America.
k. It fills the huge crater of an ancient volcano.
l. The deep and vivid color of this water is almost indescribable.

Comparison of Adjectives

291 Adjectives have **three degrees** of **comparison: positive, comparative,** and **superlative.**

292 The **positive degree** expresses a quality without comparison:

Joe is *tall.*

293 The **comparative degree** expresses a higher or lower degree than the positive when two persons or things are compared:

Kay is *taller* than Joan.   Joan is *less talkative* than Kay.

294 The **superlative degree** is the highest or lowest degree when more than two persons or things are compared:

Bob is the *tallest* boy in the club.   He is also the *least talkative* member.

295 Comparison is indicated in three ways:

a. By adding *er* or *est* to the positive degree: *large—larger—largest.*
b. By prefixing *more* and *most* or *less* and *least: graceful—more graceful—most graceful; practical—less practical—least practical.*
c. By irregular inflection: *bad—worse—worst.*

FORMS OF COMPARISON

Positive	Comparative	Superlative
long	longer	longest
beautiful	more beautiful	most beautiful
beautiful	less beautiful	least beautiful
much	more	most

296 Use the comparative degree (293), not the superlative, in comparing two objects:

He is the *older* of the two boys.   She is the *more gifted* of the two.

♦ The familiar expression, "Put your *best* foot forward," is correct as an idiomatic construction.

297 Certain adjectives that express **absolute qualities** do not logically, and in the strictest sense, admit of comparison; but many good writers do compare them regularly while others use *more nearly* and *most nearly* as an alternative use. The words *unique, perfect, square, straight, endless, dead, perpendicular* are in this group:

This is the *most* perfect rose. (questionable as **redundant**)
This is the *most nearly* perfect rose. (preferred as **logically acceptable**)

However, when such words are not used with their basic literal meaning, they may be compared:

This is the *deadest* party I ever attended.

298   The comparative is used with *than* because only two things (whether individuals or groups) are involved:

The new machine runs *faster* than the old one. (Two groups are compared.)

When comparing something with the rest of the class of things to which it belongs, use *other, else,* or some such word:

John works faster than any *other* boy in school. (John is compared with the rest of the boys.)

Exercise 2.24   Comparison of Adjectives.
For each of the following furnish the comparative or superlative form of the adjective in parentheses.

EXAMPLE: Eric does (good) work than Jeff.   *better*

a. That is the (colorful) of the two birds.
b. Did he say that iron is (heavy) than lead?
c. Who has the (many) friends, Carl or Bruce?
d. He is the (courteous) person that I know.
e. Which of the twins does the (good) work?
f. Which of your feet is (large)?
g. Which of the five children has the (many) marbles?
h. John is (athletic) than any other member of his family.
i. This is the (bad) cake that I have ever eaten.
j. The (young) of the two is the (tall) and the (thin).

Usage

299   When a numeral adjective and a noun form a compound adjective, the singular form of the noun is used:

a thirty-*day* vacation, a five-*foot* fence.

300   When a plural adjective modifies a noun, as a rule the noun becomes plural:

He rode ten *miles* (not *mile*).

301   Words such as *dozen, head, score, gross,* and *hundred* retain their singular form when preceded by an adjective expressing number:

He kept three *head* of horses in his stable.

302   *This* and *that* are the only adjectives inflected for number. *This* and *that* modify singular nouns: *these* and *those,* plural nouns:

I like *this* kind of book and *these* kinds of pencils.
She prefers *those* kinds of roses and *that* kind of aster.

303 *First* and *last,* when used with adjectives that express number, are placed before the adjectives to make the meaning specific:

Omit the *last* ten pages (*not* the ten *last* pages).

304 When two or more adjectives modify the same noun, clearness requires that an article (*a, an,* or *the*) be used before the first adjective only:

a blue, gray, and white bird. (one bird)

305 When two or more adjectives modify different nouns, one expressed and the others understood (248), an article is used before each adjective:

The large and *the* small house are mine. (two houses)

306 *Less* indicates amount; *fewer* denotes number:

We hope for *less* rain this month.
Fewer than twenty girls played ball.

307 The article *a* or *an* is not used after *kind of* or *sort of:*

What *kind of* (not *kind of a*) book is that?

308 When two or more nouns are used to refer to the same person or thing, an article should be used before the first noun only:

The teacher and mayor (one person) of the town was loved by everyone.

309 When nouns used together refer to different persons or things, an article should be used before each noun:

The teacher and *the* minister are popular. (two persons)

310 In comparison use *so* instead of *as* after a negative such as *not*:

She is not *so* tall as Jane. (*So* is used in the negative statement.)
She is *as* tall as Mary. (*As* is used in the positive statement.)

311 Do not use an adjective as an adverb. Do not use *sure* for *surely, real* for *really, some* for *somewhat, different* for *differently:*

She *surely* (not *sure*) is busy.
He was *really* (not *real*) pleased to help.

312 Remember that verbs of the senses, such as *smell, taste, feel, look,* are generally completed by adjectives, not by adverbs:

He looks *tired.* (**adjective**, 180*d*, 278, 289)

313 After any words used as linking verbs (179), the adjective (278, 289) form, not the adverb, should be used: *seem, become, appear, prove, remain, keep, stay, continue.*

314 The verbs *turn* and *grow* used in the sense of *become* are followed by an adjective:

The leaves turn *red.*   The clouds grow *dark.*

315 The suffix *-like* may be added to many nouns to form an adjective: *home-like, lifelike, swanlike.*

However, *-like* should not be added indiscriminately to those adjectives for which a word with this meaning already exists.

Incorrect: The flame was *bluelike.*
Correct: The flame was *bluish.*

Exercise 2.25   Using Adjectives.

Rewrite each of the following sentences, making all necessary corrections in the use of adjectives.

EXAMPLE: The tall boy has less ambition than any $\overset{other}{\wedge}$ applicant in the room.

a. The warmed-over coffee smelled good, but it tasted bitterly.
b. Mr. Kemp is planning to go to California for a ten-days vacation.
c. Hal is not as tall as Bob, but he is the heaviest of the two.
d. There were not as many students taking German last year as this year.
e. I polished Dad's car, and now it is shinier than any car on our street.
f. I have heard that the last three stories in this book are great.
g. The room looks beautifully with the furniture arranged differently.
h. We are glad that there are less car accidents happening every week.
i. Both perfumes smell sweetly, but this is the sweetest of the two.
j. I have read both books, and I think *Beyond the Bridge* is the best.
k. He is not so tall as Ted, but he is the best basketball player of the two.
l. A Swiss boy, a Korean girl, and a Italian boy are exchange students here.

ADVERBS

316 An **adverb** may modify a **verb** (170-180), an **adjective** (275-280), another **adverb**, a **verbal** (198-201), a **preposition** (341-346), a **conjunction** (365-369), or occasionally a **substantive** (47, 61):

She sings *beautifully.* (*Beautifully* modifies the verb *sings.*)
He is a *very* great orator. (*Very* modifies the adjective *great.*)
She smiled *rather* sadly. (*Rather* modifies the adverb *sadly.*)
By working *faithfully,* she won success. (*Faithfully* modifies the gerund *working.*)
The little boy, smiling *happily,* ran to meet his father. (*Happily* modifies the participle *smiling.*)
She has learned to write *clearly.* (*Clearly* modifies the infinitive *to write.*)
He was *almost* under the tree. (*Almost* modifies the preposition *under.*)
She came *just* before I left. (*Just* modifies the conjunction *before.*)
Nearly all of them were lost. (*Nearly* modifies the indefinite pronoun *all,* see 139.)
The *newly* rich were not invited. (*Newly* modifies the noun equivalent *rich;* see 61.)

♦ Not all grammarians agree and some state that an adverb may not modify the preposition alone, but modifies the entire phrase introduced by the preposition. They also say that an adverb may not modify a conjunction, but modifies the clause introduced by it. Therefore in the sentences above it could be said that *almost* modifies the phrase *under the tree,* and that *just* modifies the clause *before I left.* Sometimes an adverb appears to modify an entire sentence and is therefore called a **sentence adverb:**

Evidently, he doesn't care what we think.

The adverb may be a single word, a phrase (8), or a clause (9):

The child sang *joyfully.* (**word**)
The child sang *with joy.* (**phrase**)
The child sang *because he was happy.* (**clause**)

The addition of adverb modifiers gives life to expression, as is shown by the illustration below (see also 275):

The president spoke.
The new president spoke *briefly* but *enthusiastically* about the plans for the coming year.

Such expressions as *one by one, by and by, now and then,* and *little by little* are called **phrasal adverbs.**

317 According to their use in a sentence, adverbs may be grouped into three classes: **simple, interrogative,** and **conjunctive.**

318 A **simple adverb** is a simple modifier:

She spoke *kindly.*

319 An **interrogative adverb** is used in asking a question:

Where have you been?

320 A **conjunctive adverb** is used to connect independent clauses (367, 397). Some common conjunctive adverbs are: *accordingly, also, anyhow, besides, consequently, however, moreover, nevertheless, otherwise, still, then, therefore, yet:*

Joe did not like the course; *nevertheless,* he worked hard and made a good grade.
Joe did not like the course; he worked hard, *nevertheless,* and made a good grade.

A semicolon (490) is used between clauses joined by a conjunctive adverb whether the adverb begins the second clause, as in the first sentence above, or is used within it, as in the second sentence.

321 **Simple adverbs** are divided into classes: adverbs of **manner, time, place, degree,** and **number.**

322 Adverbs of **manner** indicate how the action takes place:

He walked *proudly.*

323 Adverbs of **time** indicate when the action takes place:

Fred left *yesterday.*

324 Adverbs of **place** indicate where the action takes place:

Some of my friends were *there.*

325 Adverbs of **degree** indicate how much or to what extent:

She seemed *rather* confident.

326 Adverbs of **number** indicate order or how many times:

He arrived *first.*   He came only *once.*

327 Adverbs, like adjectives, have **three degrees** of **comparison** (291-295)— **positive, comparative,** and **superlative:** *slowly–more slowly–most slowly.* In general, this is possible only for adverbs of manner.

Exercise 2.26.   Recognizing Adjectives and Adverbs.
Copy over the following sentences, drawing one line under each adjective and circling each adverb. Do not mark articles and possessives.

EXAMPLE: Learning is not <u>accidental</u>; it is (usually) the result of <u>conscientious</u>
effort.

a. Frequently students carelessly overlook great opportunities.
b. The really intelligent person watches continually for opportunity.
c. The often quoted maxim "Opportunity knocks but once" is all too true.
d. It is also true that a good education is the greatest opportunity of all.
e. It is clear to the aware student that success is a return for an honest effort in any difficult task.
f. The attitude a student develops now toward doing an assigned task will probably remain with that student.
g. One's personal work habits generally last an entire lifeime.
h. The value of learning to perform one's tasks promptly, neatly, and to the best of one's ability is immeasurable.
i. A student's record of accomplishment (or nonaccomplishment) follows the student out of the school and into the mainstream of the working world.
j. Prospective employers generally look at one's past record to determine if that person takes pride in a job well done.
k. They consult one's school records to find out if one learns quickly, accepts responsibility willingly, and works well with one's peers.

Usage

328 Do not use the adjective *most* for the adverb *almost* (628):

It seems that *almost* (not *most*) all the students are here. (See 316 and 325)

329 *Good* is an adjective; *well* is usually an adverb. Do not confuse these words:

He writes *well* (not *good*).   The apple tastes *good*. (See 289)

When it means "not sick," *well* is an adjective:

I am glad he is *well* again.

330 Do not use these nonstandard, dialectal adverbial expressions: *anywheres, nowheres, somewheres, nowhere near, muchly.*

331 When *very* or *too* modifies a past participle (201), it should be accompanied by another adverb, such as *greatly* or *much.*

John was very *much* excited.

♦ The adverb *very* is overused as an intensifier and should be avoided. *Very excited* is colloquially acceptable.

332 Do not use such words as *up* and *of* unnecessarily:

Let's *connect* (not *connect up*) these wires.
They lost *all* (not *all of*) their money.

333 *Kind of* and *sort of* should not be misused for such adverbs as *rather* and *somewhat,* when this is the meaning intended:

She was *somewhat* (not *sort of*) surprised.

334 Do not use *some* as an adverb in careful writing. Use *somewhat:*

He is *somewhat* better today.

335 *Thisaway* and *thataway* are dialectal forms:

Dialectal: The robbers went *thataway.*
Standard: The robbers went *that way.*

336 Do not use two negatives to express one negative idea; for example, do not use *not* with *hardly, scarcely, only, neither, never, no one, nobody, nothing, no,* or *none:*

There was *no one* at home (*not* There wasn't no one at home).

♦ As a rule, place *not* directly before the word it modifies:

Not every soldier can be a general (*not* Every soldier cannot be a general).

♦ Some apparently double negatives are correct:

She was not *unwilling* to
help.

No one liked the play, *not* even
Jane.

337 Use *from* after *different* and *differently* (361):

He thinks differently *from* (not *than*) you.

338 Do not use any word between the parts of an **infinitive** (199, 235) if it results in an awkward expression:

Awkward: He told me to *not* sell the book.
Correct: He told me *not* to sell the book.

339 Do not misuse the adjective *easy* for the adverb *easily:*

We can finish *easily* (not *easy*) by noon.

♦ Certain phrases, such as *take it easy, go easy,* are colloquially acceptable.

340 The position of the adverb is rather flexible in English sentences, but sometimes the position of an adverb will change the meaning of a sentence:

He *only* seems interested in reading. (He is really not interested.)
He seems interested *only* in reading. (Reading is apparently his only interest.)

Exercise 2.27   Using Adverbs.
Copy the following sentences, crossing out any misused adverbs and making the corrections above the line.

       somewhat   *deliberately*
EXAMPLE: He is ~~some~~ older now and moves very ~~deliberate~~.

  a. Most of the young players feel kind of bad about missing the game.
  b. She sure writes real well for one with so little training.
  c. I thought our new shoes were alike, but yours are different than mine.
  d. Although the car ran good, we drove down the highway very careful.
  e. We were sure surprised that the leaves had changed color so sudden.
  f. Helen feels badly because she is kind of behind in her studying.
  g. Katie speaks French most as good as a Parisian would speak.
  h. This movie is some different than the book from which it was adapted.
  i. Don't you think the governor talked good on the television program?
  j. Ed wasn't never able to get from gym to Spanish class before the period began.

PREPOSITIONS

341 **A preposition** (44) is a word or a word group that shows the relation between its object (106) and some other word in the sentence:

The eagle soared *above* the peak. (*Above* is a preposition; *peak* is the object of the preposition. The two together form a prepositional phrase.)

♦ A word ordinarily used as a preposition may be used as a simple adverb (316, 318) when it has no object, or it may become part of a verb:

We have met *before*. (**adverb**)
John arrived *before* dinner. (**preposition**)
Send *in* the applicant. Send the applicant *in*. He was sent *in*. (**adverb**)

342 Although prepositions are variously classified, it is sufficient to know four general classes: **simple, compound, participial,** and **phrasal.**

343 A **simple preposition** is made up of one word: *by, for, in, with, on.*

344 A **compound preposition** is made up of two words used as one: *without, upon, into, before, inside.*

345 A **participial preposition** is the present participle of certain verbs used with the function of a preposition: *regarding, excepting, respecting, barring.*

346 A **phrasal preposition** is a phrase used as a preposition: *in spite of, in accordance with, with regard to, from below, over against.*

347 Some of the words most frequently used as prepositions are *aboard, about, above, across, after, against, along, amid, among, around, at, before, behind, below, beneath, beside, between, beyond, by, down, during, except, for, from, in, into, of, off, on, out of, outside, over, round, round about, since, through, throughout, to, unto, under, underneath, up, upon, with, within,* and *without.*

348 A preposition and its object (with the modifiers of the object) form a phrase (8) which has the use of an adjective (275) when it modifies a noun or a pronoun, and the use of an adverb (316) when it modifies a verb, adjective, or an adverb:

The tree *in the park* is an oak. (**adjective phrase** modifying *tree*)
We walked *beside the river*. (**adverb phrase** modifying *walked*)

♦ Some linguists state that a prepositional phrase may be used as a noun (47, 61). The following is an example:

At the door was where he left them.

♦ When a pronoun appears in the compound object of a preposition, the pronoun should be in the objective case (153):

The play was written by John and *me*.

Exercise 2.28   Prepositional Phrases.
Copy the following sentences, underlining each prepositional phrase. Then

circle the word each phrase modifies, and—after the sentence—indicate whether the phrase is used as an adjective or an adverb.

EXAMPLE: The (girl) at the door is Jane.—*adjective*

a. He spoke with much enthusiasm.
b. Everyone waited impatiently for the announcement.
c. The car at the curb is mine.
d. The old ship slowly sank beneath the waves.
e. The boy's dog waited patiently outside the gate.
f. The explorers saw many lakes with sandy beaches.
g. Do you know the woman at the desk?
h. We walked through the old garden.
i. The basketball coach always strives for our improvement.
j. The forest ranger's patrol plane flew above the hills.
k. A beech tree stood between the two houses.
l. Louise's mother admired the fir trees along the roadside.
m. They sat beside the little stream.
n. A valley lies beyond the mountain.
o. Don has a large collection of stamps.
p. Ginger jumped recklessly into the deep pool.
q. There were some vacation cabins with wide verandas.
r. Eileen read several books about the great nineteenth-century poets.
s. The fish in the pond are wary.
t. Henry swam across the pool.

Exercise 2.29   Placing Prepositional Phrases.

Rewrite the following sentences, reordering the modifying phrases so that the sense is clear. Underline the word that the phrase modifies.

EXAMPLE: We need a person to work on this project with experience.

We need a <u>person</u> with experience to work on this project.

a. She told me about the accident she saw in her letter.
b. You need someone to carry that load with a strong back.
c. We held a pep meeting before the football game began in the auditorium.
d. The man was carried with a broken leg on a stretcher.
e. Last week we studied about germs in our science class.
f. The boy chased the cat with a freckled face.
g. Mary invited me to the picnic over the telephone.
h. Henry arrived after the game had started in great haste.
i. They sat and watched the parade on the front porch.
j. Our car is in the garage with a broken axle.

Exercise 2.30. Pronouns in Prepositional Phrases.

Copy the following sentences, underlining each preposition and selecting the proper pronoun form.

EXAMPLE: Paul brought the sick dog <u>to</u> Carl and **I** / (me).

a. Steve and I sat behind Betty and **she** / **her**.
b. Elaine and Tom often sit beside Paul and **I** / **me**.
c. He explained the new rules to **we** / **us** players.
d. Was that letter from Manuel or **he** / **him**?
e. It's almost time for **we** / **us** students to start studying.
f. The tennis match was between Anita and **I** / **me**.
g. Was that wise remark about Floyd and **I** / **me**?
h. The mayor presented a silly key to **we** / **us**.

Usage

349   There are some 284 words and phrases in English used as prepositions and prepositional phrases. The following sections (350-364) illustrate a number of the distinctions to be made in correct usage. Modern dictionaries carefully indicate the idiomatic distinctions to be made in formal expression.

350   One may *agree to* a thing and *agree with* a person:

   I agree to the plan.   You *agree* with me.

351   One may be *angry at* or *about* a thing and *angry with* a person:

   I was *angry at* the discourtesy.   He was *angry with* me.

352   One *arrives in* a large city, *at* a small place:

   He *arrived* in Chicago.   We *arrived at* the village.

353   *Besides* means *in addition to; beside* means *by the side of:*

   There were two boys *besides* Henry.   He sat *beside* me.

354   *Between* refers to two; *among,* to more than two:

   She divided the candy *between* the two boys.
   He threw the confetti *among* the crowd.

355   One is *accompanied by* a person, *with* a thing:

   Mabel was *accompanied by* her mother.
   The rain was *accompanied with* hail.

356   Do not use *inside of* for *within*:

   He did not finish the work *within* (not *inside of*) a week.

357   *Into* denotes entrance; *in* denotes location:

   He jumped *into* the water.   He swam *in* the river.

358   One may die *of* disease, *from* exposure, or *by* violence:

   He died *of* pneumonia.   She died *from* exposure, not *by* her
                                         own act.

359 *By* is the word to use after *follow* when referring to what follows:

The murderer was followed *by* a mob.

360 *Differ with* means *disagree in opinion; differ from* means *be unlike* or *dissimilar:*

I *differ with* you about the value of the painting.
The horses *differ* from each other in color.

361 *From* should be used with the adjective *different:*

This hat is different *from* (not *than*) that. (337)

362 One *parts from* a person, *with* a thing:

Romeo *parted from* Juliet.
The miser did not wish to *part with* his gold.

363 Do not use *in back of* for *behind:*

The garage is *behind* (not *in back of*) the house.

364 Do not use unnecessary words such as: accept *of*, off *of*, remember *of*, where *at*, where *to*.

Exercise 2.31   Using Prepositions.
Copy the following sentences, crossing out any prepositions used incorrectly and supplying correct substitutes as necessary above the line. Write **C** after any correct sentence.

with

EXAMPLE: Mr. Johnson was angry ~~at~~ Scott because he knocked the paint

off ~~of~~ the shelf.

   a. Sue differs with Sally in personality.
   b. Who besides Joe sat in back of you?
   c. Dolores's coat is different than yours.
   d. If he isn't to school, where is he at?
   e. I walked in the room and sat besides Ed.
   f. One among us was a spy.
   g. Who took the receiver off of the hook?
   h. Father will be angry at you if you don't tell him where you went to.
   i. I don't like to differ from you, but I cannot agree with the proposal.
   j. I agree with you that the property should be divided between the four of us.
   k. Someone had broken in the house and had knocked the vase off of the table.
   l. We collected the money off the others.
   m. Mother was angry at the slow service.
   n. Eileen and I walked besides the stream.
   o. My answer is different than his.
   p. I walked respectfully in back of him.

q. Ms. Harris borrowed the mower off Father.
r. Where did you go to on your vacation?
s. I was in the pool when he dived into it.
t. I was to home sitting in an easy chair.

CONJUNCTIONS

365 A **conjunction** (45) connects words or groups of words; in form it may be a single word or a group of words:

Robert *and* James are here. (a single word connecting two words)
She came *while* you were away. (a single word connecting clauses)
The teachers *as well as* the students had a good time. (a group of words used as a conjunction)

366 Although conjunctions have many classifications, it is sufficient for our purpose to note only three general classes: **coordinating, subordinating**, and **correlative**.

Relative adverbs used as conjunctions are also called **conjunctive adverbs** or **adverbial conjunctions**.

367 A **coordinating conjunction** connects two words, two phrases, or two clauses of equal rank:

Paul *and* Carl are here. (*And* connects two nouns.)
She liked to read *but* not to write (not *writing*). (*But* connects two infinitives.)

The coordinating conjunctions in most general use include *and, but, for, or, nor, yet.* The conjunctive adverbs, such as *however, then, therefore,* and *thus,* also connect independent clauses (320) when used with a semicolon.

368 A **subordinating conjunction** connects two clauses of unequal rank; that is, it joins a dependent (subordinate) clause (398) to the independent clause (397) on which it depends:

I was here *before* you came.

Some of the subordinating conjunctions are *as, as if, because, before, if, since, that, till, unless, when, where, whether.*
The relative pronouns *who, whom, whose, which, what, that,* also serve as subordinating conjunctions (135).

369 Conjunctions that are used in pairs are called **correlative conjunctions** and include *both-and, either-or, neither-nor, not only-but also.*

Neither John *nor* I will be able to come.

Exercise 2.32   Recognizing Conjunctions.
Copy the following sentences, underlining each conjunction. Above it write c

if it is a coordinating conjunction, **cor** if it is correlative, or **sub** if it is subordinate.

EXAMPLE: I have *cor* neither time *cor* nor money.

a. Sally and I deciphered the message.
b. If you see Juana, give her my regards.
c. You'll find paper and ink either on the desk or in the top drawer.
d. Father looked out but could see nothing.
e. I was late because no one awakened me.
f. Not only did he greet Ann and me, but also he called us by name.
g. I'll go with Sam or Bessie.
h. I know that you and he will try.
i. He is both secretary and treasurer.
j. Have you heard whether he is coming?
k. Send Mother or me your new address.
l. The weather should be fair and warmer.

Usage

370 Do not use *except* for *unless:*

We will play *unless* (not *except* or *without*) you object.

371 Do not use *without* for *that:*

I never meet her *that I do not* (not *without I*) admire her wit.

372 Do not use *like* for *as, as if, as though,* or *that* in formal writing:

Walk *as* (not *like*) he told you.
It seems *that* (not *like*) he should help.

373 *And etc.* for *etc.* is incorrect. *Etc.* is an abbreviation of the Latin words *et cetera,* meaning *and so forth;* therefore *and* is not needed.

374 *And, but,* and *or* are used so frequently that a piece of writing may soon become overloaded with compound sentences. Learn to use the other conjunctions for sentence variety.

375 *And, or, but,* and correlative conjunctions (369) should be used to join expressions that are parallel in form:

She liked *to stroll* on the beach and *to watch* the sea birds.
He is coming *with us* by car or *with his family* by train.

376 Most grammarians agree that the relative (conjunctive pronoun) *which* should not be used to refer to an entire clause (166):

Questionable: The traffic was heavy, *which caused me to be late.*
Better: I was late because the traffic was heavy.

377 When a subordinate conjunction (368) introduces two or more statements of equal importance, the conjunction should in most cases be repeated before each clause to make the meaning clear:

> She told me *that* she had won the prize and *that* she would return.

378 *Nor* is used with *neither* or after some negative word:

> He can *neither* read *nor* (not *or*) write.
> He cannot dive, *nor* does he like to swim.

379 After verbs of *saying, thinking,* and *feeling,* do not use *as* to replace *that:*

> I feel *that* (not *as*) I should not go.

380 Do not use *where* for *that:*

> I read in the paper *that* (not *where*) the price of wheat had advanced.

381 Do not use *if* for *whether* in formal writing:

> I do not know *whether* (not *if*) he will come.

382 Each of a pair of correlative conjunctions (369) should be placed immediately before the word it connects:

> He eats *both* meat *and* fish. (not: He *both* eats meat *and* fish.)

383 In clauses of purpose, do not use *so* for *so that* in formal use:

> He worked hard so *that* he could pay his debts.

384 Use *when* to follow *scarcely* or *hardly;* use *than* to follow the expression of a comparison:

> He had scarcely started *when* the accident happened.
> He did better *than* I expected.

385 Use *that* before a clause which follows a verb of *saying, thinking,* or *feeling* when the verb is followed by an infinitive:

> He studied hard, for he knew *that* to fail would be his ruin.

386 Do not omit *as* when it is necessary to complete a comparison:

> **Illogical:** Jane is tall, if not taller than you.
> **Logical:** Jane is *as* tall *as* you, if not taller.

Exercise 2.33   Using Conjunctions.

For each of the following select the correct conjunction from those furnished in boldface.

EXAMPLE: It looks (**as if**)/ **like** it may rain.

a. Neither rain **nor/or** snow keeps him away.
b. It seems **like/that** I was wrong.
c. Find out **if/whether** that plane took off.

d. I see **that/where** he will speak here.
e. He looks **as if/like** he is tired.
f. I won't go **except/unless** Mother agrees.
g. I did **as/like** you suggested.
h. I can't go **unless/without** I take Jill.
i. Do you know **if/whether** he has voted?
j. We could neither see **nor/or** hear.
k. Do you feel **as/that** you can help?
l. I read **that/where** Dick would be here.

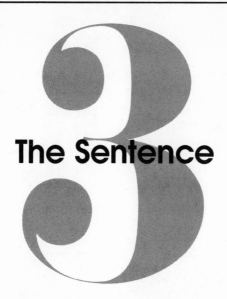

The Sentence

It has been well said that good English is lucid English. If this be true, then the speaker or writer who has mastered the English sentence in its simple and in its complex forms will have the means of self-expression with clarity and precision. In modern terms, one communicates.

Just as a carpenter studies the materials and tools in order to best build a house, we study the sentence as the tool of effective expression for our thoughts.

SENTENCE STRUCTURE AND ANALYSIS

387   A sentence must express a thought (1); therefore it must have a subject and a predicate (3, 4) either expressed or understood (5); and it may also have modifiers (7) and independent elements (12).

388   In general, sentences are made up of **words, phrases** (8), and **clauses** (9). The classification of words has been given in Chapter Two under *Parts of Speech.* Phrases and clauses are also classified in several ways.

389   A **phrase** is a group of related words used as a part of a sentence but not having a subject (3) or a predicate (4). A phrase may be a modifier (7, 8), a connective (365), or a substantive (47):

Ann came *with me.* (**modifier**)
To make a mistake is not disgraceful. (**substantive**)

The **verb phrase** (15, 41, 181, 391) is not a modifier, a connnective, nor a substantive.

390   According to **structure** there are four general classes of phrases: **prepositional, infinitive, participial,** and **gerund:**

    a.   A **prepositional phrase** includes a preposition (341, 347) and its object and modifiers of the object:

      Burns lived *among the hills.*

    b.   An **infinitive phrase** includes an infinitive and its object or complement and modifiers:

      Byron liked *to write poetry.*

    c.   A **participial phrase** includes a participle and its object and modifiers:

      The girl, *walking quickly,* joined the others.

    d.   A **gerund phrase** includes a gerund and its object and modifiers:

      Painting beautiful pictures is interesting work.

391   The **verb phrase** is a phrasal verb, that is, a verb consisting of two or more words (41).   The various forms of *be, have* and of the auxiliary verbs (*can, may, shall, will, must, ought, do*) are combined with main verb forms to make up the verb phrase.

392   According to their **use** phrases are classified as follows: **noun** (substantive), **adjective,** and **adverb.**   They are referred to by some writers as **nominal, adjectival, adverbial.**

393   A **noun phrase** may be used as a regular noun, with the exception that it is never used in the possessive case (116):

    Playing tennis is delightful exercise. (This is a gerund phrase, 390*d,* used as the subject. All gerunds are, of course, used as nouns, 200.)

♦ The following sentences illustrate other uses of gerunds as nouns:

    My favorite exercise is *swimming.* **(predicate nominative,** 96)
    Robert likes *swimming.* **(object of verb,** 102)
    We talked about *swimming.* **(object of a preposition,** 106)
    Her work, *writing stories,* is very interesting. **(apposition with the subject,** 100, 101)
    He likes his work, *teaching music.* **(apposition with object of verb)**

♦ The infinitive phrase (390*b*) has the following uses as a noun:

    To try is noble. **(subject)**
    I like *to swim.* **(direct object)**
    Her desire is *to succeed.* **(predicate nominative)**
    Her aim, *to succeed,* is worthy. **(apposition with subject)**
    I dread my task, *to sell tickets.* **(apposition with object of verb)**
    He spoke of his duty, *to work.* **(apposition with object of preposition)**

♦ The prepositional phrase (390*a*, 348) is not regularly used as a noun, but some writers consider the following as an example of such a use:

Over the fence is out.

♦ The participial phrase (390*c*) is used as an adjective and not as a noun; but the gerund is in reality a form of participle used as a noun and is sometimes called **verbal noun** or **participial noun** (56, 200).

394   An **adjective phrase** is a phrase used as an adjective (42, 275-290, 399). The prepositional phrase (390*a*), the infinitive phrase (390*b*), or the participial phrase (390*c*) may be used as an adjective:

The house *on the hill* is white. (**prepositional phrase** used as an adjective to modify *house*)

Evelyn has a great deal of work *to do*. (**infinitive phrase** used as an adjective to modify *work*)

The girl *holding the bat* is Susan. (**participial phrase** used as an adjective to modify *girl*)

395   An **adverb phrase** is a phrase used as an adverb (43, 316-326, 413). Phrases used as adverbs are generally either prepositional or infinitive:

Helen came *with Mary*. (**prepositional phrase** used as an adverb to modify *came*)

The men came *to work*. (**infinitive phrase** used as an adverb to modify *came*)

♦ A phrase may sometimes be either adverbial or adjectival:

He saw a book *on the table*.   He knew the book *on the table*.

Exercise 3.1   Use of Phrases.
Copy the following sentences on a separate sheet, underlining all of the phrases furnished here in boldface. Above each underlined phrase identify it as prepositional, infinitive, participial, or gerund, and then indicate how it is used in the sentence (i.e., noun, adjective, or adverb). Draw an arrow to the words modified by each adjective or adverb phrase.

⌒*prep–adj*   ⌒*inf–n*
EXAMPLE: Every citizen **of America** should try **to see its wonders**.

a. Carlsbad Caverns in New Mexico was discovered **by Jim White**, a cowhand.
b. **Finding the caverns** was perhaps the most important event **in his life**.
c. **During the Coolidge administration**, this region was made **into a national monument**.
d. Later, in 1930, the caverns and the region **surrounding them** became a national park.
e. The caverns have been the subject **of constant exploration**, but no one yet knows how far they may extend **under the mountains**.

f. Each evening **in summer** millions of bats come **from the cave** and return at dawn.
g. A wave of flights, **beginning at sunset**, lasts about an hour.
h. Tourists **in great numbers** come **to witness this mass flight**.
i. A small fee **for guide service** is charged each adult **entering the caverns**.
j. **To reach the lunchroom** one walks **for about two hours**.
k. Visitors **not bringing their lunches** may buy food **in the lunchroom**.
l. **Eating lunch** deep **in the caverns** is a very enjoyable part **of the trip**.
m. Then visitors enter the Big Room, the most fantastic and beautiful part **of the caverns**.
n. A delightful way **to spend a vacation** is **visiting our national parks**.

Exercise 3.2   Writing Stronger Sentences.
Two simple sentences may frequently be combined into a stronger sentence by using phrases or conjunctions. Combine each pair of the following sentences as directed in the parentheses. (Correct answers may vary.)

EXAMPLE: (appositive) Hal Robert is my cousin. He went to Brazil last year.

> *Hal Roberts, my cousin, went to Brazil last year.*

a. (gerund subject) Claire loves to sing western songs. This is her favorite hobby.
b. (infinitive) Patsy drove to the station. She went to meet a Canadian friend.
c. (appositive) Meg Ford is president of our bank. She is a fine administrator.
d. (participial phrase) That package is yours. It is wrapped in brown paper.
e. (compound subject) Bill plays table tennis. Christine plays table tennis.
f. (compound object) My older brother plays the piano. He also plays the violin.
g. (appositive) Emily Dickinson wrote many lyrics. She was an American poet.
h. (gerund predicate nominative) Mr. Hardy writes love songs. This is his favorite hobby.
i. (prepositional phrase) Ed went to the show. He went with Lucille.
j. (participial phrase) That child is lost. He is standing at the corner.

396   A **clause** is a group of words which contains a subject (3) and a predicate (4). It is usually considered a part of a sentence; but when it is capable of standing alone, it is equivalent to a simple sentence (21). Words are sometimes properly omitted from the clause (10):

> Mary is the girl *who wrote the letter.*
> The officer said, *"Stop."* (*You*, the **subject**, is omitted here.)

Clauses as parts of a sentence are classified as **independent** (called also **principal clause** or **main clause**) and **dependent** or **subordinate**.

397 The **independent clause** is one that makes complete sense when standing alone and that is grammatically complete.

The students deliver papers before they come to school. (The clause *The students deliver papers* could stand alone, as it expresses a complete thought.)

398 A **dependent** (subordinate) **clause** is used as a part of speech in a sentence and usually does not make sense when standing alone:

The students deliver papers *before they come to school.* (The clause *before they come to school* is incomplete in sense when standing alone; here it is used as an adverb and modifies the verb in the main clause.)

399 A dependent clause may be used as a **noun,** an **adjective,** or an **adverb.** The **noun clause** may be used in a variety of ways. These uses are illustrated in sections 400–407. **Adjective clauses** and **adverb clauses** are explained in sections 408 and 409.

Noun Clause

400 The noun clause is used as subject (3) of a sentence:

What she thought seemed important to him.

401 The noun clause is used as direct object of a verb (6):

Don said *that he tried.*

♦ An infinitive (199) construction which often replaces a *that* clause is sometimes called an **infinitive clause:**

John asked *me to stay.* (This is equivalent to *John asked that I should stay;* therefore *me to stay* is a noun clause, of which *me* is the subject—the subject of an infinitive is always in the objective case—and *to stay* is the predicate. *Me to stay* is the direct object of *asked.*)

402 The noun clause is used as object of a preposition (106):

We talked about *what we would do.*

403 The noun clause is used as predicate nominative (96):

The fact is *that she won the prize.*

404 The noun clause is used in apposition (100) with the subject:

The report *that she won* is correct.

405 The noun clause is used in apposition (101) with the object of a verb:

You made the statement *that she won.*

406 The noun clause is used in apposition with object of a preposition:

We thought of his answer, *"I do not care what you say."*

407   The noun clause is used in apposition (100) with the predicate nominative:

The clearest evidence is the fact *that she won.*

Exercise 3.8   Noun Clauses.

On a separate sheet write the noun clause for each of the following sentences. Then indicate how the clause is used within that sentence (that is, as subject, predicate nominative, direct object, object of a preposition, or appositive).

EXAMPLE: I don't know what she will do now.

what she will do now—direct object

a. I'll give the billfold to whoever can identify it.
b. The fact that you have talent should inspire you.
c. My big problem is how I can earn enough money.
d. Whatever you want will have our approval.
e. The rumor that it was a fatal accident was untrue.
f. The teacher asked why we were late to school.
g. Do you know who will be elected?
h. Whomever you nominate will be elected.
i. The question now is what we should do next.
j. Have you heard who won?
k. The truth is that I can't decide.
l. How we spend our leisure time is very important.
m. The fact is that many of us waste valuable time.
n. We alone can determine what we will achieve.
o. Our achievement must start from where we are.
p. Whether we fail or succeed rests upon ourselves.
q. The reason for his failure is the fact that he loafed.
r. We wondered why we had not succeeded.
s. I realized that I had not really applied myself.
t. We usually judge people by what they do.

Adjective Clause

408   An **adjective clause** is a clause used as an adjective (275, 414). The adjective clause may be introduced by a relative pronoun (135), a relative adverb (such as *where, when, while, why*), or subordinate conjunction (368). The relative adverbs are also classed as subordinating conjunctions, but when used to introduce adjective clauses, they have antecedents. In some instances, the word which connects the clause is omitted:

This is the book *that I bought.* (adjective clause, modifying *book,* introduced by the pronoun *that)*

That is the place *where we saw him.* (adjective clause, modifying *place,* introduced by the relative adverb *where)*

Is that the girl *we met yesterday?* (adjective clause omitting the introductory pronoun)

♦ Whether the introductory word is expressed or not, it must be considered as a part of the clause. The omitted word in the last example is *whom*, and it must be considered the object of *met.*

Adverb Clause

409 An **adverb clause** is a clause used as an adverb (316–326, 414). The adverb clause is introduced by a subordinating conjunction (368):

When we had finished our difficult task, we drove through the park. (The subordinating conjunction *when* introduces the adverb clause which modifies the verb *drove.*)

The adverb clause which stands at the beginning of a sentence is followed by a comma (497) unless it is very short and cannot be misread. A comma is usually not used when the main clause (397) stands first:

When we had finished our difficult task, we drove through the park.
After we left the lights were turned on.

We stayed at home *because the weather was unpleasant.* (The subordinating conjunction *because* introduces the adverb clause which modifies the verb *stayed.*)

Exercise 3.4   Clause Modifiers.
Using a separate sheet, list each of the clause modifiers present in the following passage. Then indicate whether it is used as an adjective or an adverb.

EXAMPLE: Name the states through which you have traveled.

<u>*through which you have traveled–adjective*</u>

  a. Chita and I visited Yosemite National Park last summer when her parents lent us their car.
  b. The part of the park which visitors like best is Yosemite Valley.
  c. This valley, which occupies but eight square miles, is only a small part of the park area.
  d. The part of the park above the rim of the valley is not so well known because it was not open to motorists at first.
  e. There are now roads which make travel in the park easy.
  f. Chita and I first saw El Capitan, a towering mass of exposed granite, one of the largest in the world, because we entered from the west.
  g. The valley through which we traveled has a large number of waterfalls.
  h. The Service rangers who are stationed at the park told us the story of its geologic history.
  i. We would not leave the region until we had seen the valley from Glacier Point.
  j. From the point, when we looked into the valley, the automobiles there seemed mere specks.
  k. Until we had seen the waterfalls of the park, we could not imagine their beauty.

l. Upper Yosemite Falls has a drop which is nine times the height of Niagara Falls.

m. Ribbon Falls, which is the highest fall in the park, has a drop of 1612 feet.

n. Chita and I have a deeper appreciation for our world's natural beauty since we have seen Yosemite.

o. We told our friends to visit the park because it is so beautiful. ·

Exercise 3.5   Phrases and Clauses.

For each of the following determine whether the expression in boldface is a prepositional phrase or a dependent clause. Then indicate whether it is used as an adjective or an adverb.

EXAMPLE: The rocket passed **through the thick clouds.**

> *Prep. phrase—adverb*

a. The drive **through the Rocky Mountains** was beautiful.
b. **When I have saved enough money,** I'll buy a car.
c. **After I played tennis,** I lay down to rest.
d. The house **in which he was born** is still standing.
e. The cast had a party **after the final performance.**
f. I'll wash the dishes **after the guests leave.**
g. **In the old vacant house** the robbers had hidden the money.
h. You should read the story **that I read.**
i. Mercedes is the girl **in the green sweater and skirt.**
j. The boy **who sang** is on the football team.

SENTENCE FORM

410 A sentence (1, 387) must have a subject and a predicate (2) and it may have other parts, such as objects, complements, and modifiers of all types (1-19). As to form, a sentence may be classified as **simple** (21), **compound** (22), **complex** (23), and **compound–complex** (20, 416). The **simple sentence** must have but **one** independent clause (397). The subject (3) or the predicate (4) or both (19) may be compound; and it may contain any number of phrases, but no dependent clause (398):

The man at the window sent a ticket for John. (This simple sentence contains two phrases.)

John and Melba bought baseballs and bats and packed them in cartons. (This simple sentence contains a compound subject, a compound predicate, a compound direct object, and one phrase.)

Although there are certain parts (2) necessary to every sentence, all sentences are made up of words and groups of words. We have noted the classification of words as parts of speech (38-386), and the classification of groups of words as phrases and clauses (389–409). In the study of the relationships of the parts of the sentence, there are three methods used by grammarians— **parsing, analyzing, diagramming**—to state or show these relationships.

411 **Parsing** is to give a grammatical description of each word in a sentence by naming the part of speech to which it belongs, its modification, and its function in the sentence.

Mary paints beautiful pictures.

Mary is a proper noun (55), feminine gender (65), third person (72), singular number (74), nominative case (95), subject of the verb *paints*.

Paints is a regular transitive verb (171, 174), indicative mood (187), present tense (191), active voice (184), third person (72), singular number (74) to agree (197) with its subject *Mary.*

Beautiful is a descriptive adjective (279), positive degree (292), and modifies the noun *pictures.*

Pictures is a common noun (54), neuter gender (66), third person (72), plural number (75), objective case (102), object of the verb *paints.*

412 **Analyzing a sentence** is to state the relation of the parts of the sentence to each other:

The little child liked the roses in the garden.

This is a simple declarative sentence (21, 25).

The little child is the complete subject (14); *child* is the simple subject (13); *the* and *little* are adjectives modifying *child. Liked the roses in the garden* is the complete predicate (16); *liked,* the simple predicate (15), is completed by the object *roses* (102). The object (6) is modified by the adjective *the* and the adjective phrase (394) *in the garden.*

413 **Diagramming a sentence** is to make a visual picture of the word relationships in it. Other diagrams of the simple sentence are given under 4, 6, 7, 19, 96, 100, 105, 265, 266, 269.

DIAGRAM—A simple sentence (21) with a *prepositional phrase* (390*a*) used as an adjective (394):

The book *on the desk* is blue.

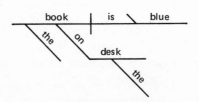

DIAGRAM—A simple sentence with *a prepositional phrase* used as an adverb (395):

A dog ran *under the fence.*

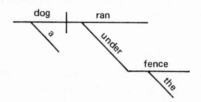

414   A **complex sentence** (23) has but **one** independent clause (397) and one or more dependent clauses (398):

Ruth left *when I arrived. (Ruth left* is an **independent clause.** *When I arrived* is a **dependent clause** which modifies the verb *left* as an adverb, 409).

This is the girl *who wrote the story that won the prize. (This is the girl* is an independent clause. *(Who wrote the story* is a **dependent clause** that modifies the noun *girl* as an adjective, 408. *That won the prize* is a **dependent clause** that modifies *story* as an adjective.)

The analysis of a complex sentence is similar to that of the simple sentence:

Bob saw the girl who wrote the story. (This is a complex sentence. *Bob saw the girl* is the main, or independent, clause, of which *Bob* is the subject, *saw* is the verb, and *girl* is the direct object. The dependent clause is *who wrote the story; who* is the subject of the dependent clause, *wrote* is the verb, and *story* is the direct object.   The dependent clause is an adjective (408), and it modifies the noun *girl.)*

DIAGRAM—A complex sentence with an *adjective clause* (408) introduced by a *relative pronoun* (135) used as *object:*

I saw the horse *which you bought.*

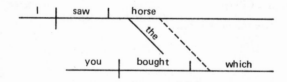

DIAGRAM—A complex sentence with an *adjective clause* introduced by a *relative pronoun* (135) used as *subject:*

The girl *who sat beside me* is my cousin.

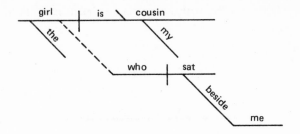

DIAGRAM—A complex sentence with an *adjective clause* introduced by a *relative adverb* (408):

That is the place *where we saw the deer.*

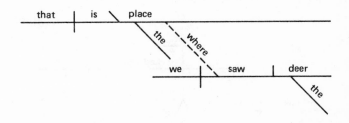

DIAGRAM—A complex sentence with an *adverb clause* (409) introduced by the *subordinating conjunction* (368) *if:*

He will win *if we help him.*

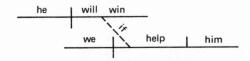

DIAGRAM—A complex sentence with an *adverb clause* introduced by the *subordinating conjunction* (368) *when:*

Mother met us *when we arrived.*

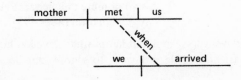

DIAGRAM—A complex sentence with a *noun clause* used as *subject* (400):

That you succeed is the truth.

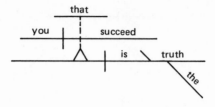

DIAGRAM—A complex sentence with a *noun clause* used as the *object* of a verb (401):

My mother said *that he had won the prize.*

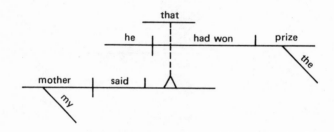

DIAGRAM—A complex sentence with a *noun clause* used as *predicate nominative* or *subjective complement* (403):

The truth is *that he bought the house.*

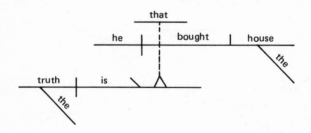

415   **A compound sentence** (22) has **two** or **more** independent clauses (397) joined by conjunctions (365–369) or by punctuation (489, 495) or by both.

The little girl went to school, but her brother stayed at home.

The short, friendly little girl went to school; but her brother stayed at home.

The little girl went to school; her brother stayed at home.

When there are no other commas (first example) used in a compound sentence, a comma is placed before the conjunction (495). But when one is used, then the comma is often replaced by the semicolon (second example). When the conjunction is not used (third example), a semicolon (489) separates the clauses. The two clauses of the sentence, being independent (397), might stand alone as sentences. But when an independent clause is changed into a sentence, it ceases to be a clause, for a clause by definition is a part of a sentence:

The little girl went to school. Her brother stayed at home. (two simple sentences)

The compound sentence is analyzed in the same way as simple sentences except that the connecting words are mentioned. Every independent clause is practically equivalent to a simple sentence, and a compound sentence may have any number of independent clauses:

The little girl went to school; her brother stayed at home; her father went to his office. (three clauses connected by semicolons, 489)

DIAGRAM—A *compound* sentence:

John goes to college, but Mark stays at home.

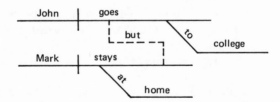

416 If either independent clause of a compound sentence has a subordinate clause (398), the sentence is called **compound-complex** or **complex-compound**:

When Henry lost the race, he was disappointed; but he was not discouraged.

DIAGRAM—A *compound-complex* sentence:

He lost the knife that he bought, but he may find it.

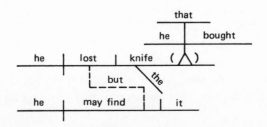

Exercise 3.6   Classifying Sentences.

Copy each of the following sentences on a separate sheet, underlining each independent clause and putting parentheses around each dependent clause. Then classify each sentence as simple, compound, complex, or compound-complex.

EXAMPLE: Our country has many historic shrines, and we should visit these

(when we can).*—compound–complex*

a. The Lincoln Memorial is one of our most impressive buildings.
b. This is a building which is located in Potomac Park, Washington.
c. Henry Bacon designed this beautiful structure, and the cornerstone was laid in 1915.
d. This memorial is built upon a slope, and it is surrounded by open spaces.
e. As you approach the building, you quickly appreciate its rare beauty.
f. Although it is simple in plan, it is impressive in size, and it is strikingly beautiful.
g. It is constructed of white Colorado marble, pink Tennessee marble, and Indiana limestone.
h. In the colonnade around the hall are columns which represent the states at the time of Lincoln's death.
i. Above the colonnade are the names of the first forty-eight states that were admitted to the union.
j. When you pass through a row of columns, you enter the center hall.
k. In this hall the sculptured figure of Lincoln is seated, and the interior is lighted by a skylight.
l. This figure was carved by Daniel Chester French, and it is deeply impressive.
m. The eyes look toward the Washington Monument and the Capitol.
n. In the face of the statue one can read the character which endeared Lincoln to the world.
o. The inner ceiling here is supported by bronze beams, which are encased in thin slabs of marble.
p. On one wall is carved the speech that Lincoln gave at Gettysburg.
q. In the north hall is carved the Second Inaugural Address, and here are paintings that represent Unity, Fraternity, and Charity.
r. This is a place which many sightseers visit.
s. If you visit this shrine, it will make you love your country more.
t. Men everywhere are indebted to Lincoln because he sought liberty and justice for all.

Exercise 3.7   Sentence Sense.

For each of the following determine whether the group of words is a complete sentence, an incomplete sentence, or two sentences incorrectly written as one.

EXAMPLE: Sitting at the tables in the study hall.—*incomplete*

a. Cheering wildly, we watched Hex make a touchdown.
b. Working, planning, and hoping that a college education would be possible.
c. Bring your new tennis racket to school tomorrow.
d. Because she had worked so long and so faithfully at perfecting her butter-fly stroke.
e. It was the most thrilling game of the season our team played well.
f. Although the work was difficult, Bill completed the job on time.
g. Went fishing with Henry and Joe last Saturday.
h. We will meet again on Wednesday, Jorge Gōmez will preside.
i. When will the performance begin?
j. While we waited impatiently for the big game to begin.

SENTENCE STYLE

417   Sentences are also classified as to the arrangement of their material as **periodic**, **loose**, and **balanced**.

418   A **periodic sentence** is one in which the main thought is not given until the end of the sentence is reached. This type of sentence is not grammatically complete until the last word. It lends emphasis:

Today, as never before in the history of the world, we need leadership.

♦ A compound sentence as a whole cannot be periodic, but its parts may be periodic.

419   A **loose sentence** gives the main thought and then adds details. It is the rambling type of expression, much used in conversation:

Lancelot returned with Guinevere in the spring when the flowers were in bloom and the world seemed full of gladness.

420   A **balanced sentence** has two parts which are alike in construction. The thoughts in the two parts may be either in agreement or in contrast:

He told his story at home, and then he repeated it at school.
He was always industrious, but he was never successful.

Variety

421   VARIETY IN SENTENCE STRUCTURE   One form of sentence may be just as effective as another, but any form becomes monotonous when it is used too frequently. Valuable practice can be had by expressing similar ideas in sentences of different form:

a. **Simple:** Mary Jones, the efficient president of our class, is an excellent musician. (An appositive, 101, is used.)

b. **Complex**: Mary Jones, who is the efficient president of our class, is an excellent musician. (A dependent, 398, nonrestrictive clause, 499, is used.)

c. **Compound** with a conjunction (415): Mary Jones is the efficient president of our class, and she is also an excellent musician. (A comma, 495, precedes the conjunction.)

d. **Compound** without a conjunction (415): Mary Jones is the efficient president of our class; she is also an excellent musician. (A semicolon, 489, separates the independent clauses.)

e. **Compound-complex** (416): Mary Jones, who is the president of our class, is a very efficient officer; and she is also an excellent musician. (For punctuation, see 489, 491.)

f. **Two simple sentences** (410): Mary Jones is the efficient president of our class. She is also a very good musician.

g. **Three simple sentences**: Mary Jones is the president of our class. She is a very efficient officer. She is also an excellent musician. (Short sentences give emphasis to expression, but they tend to become monotonous, 449.)

Exercise 3.8   Writing Compound Sentences.
Make each pair of simple sentences into a compound sentence, carefully picking your conjunction and punctuation. (Correct answers may vary.)

EXAMPLE: Fred is a brilliant student. He does not like history.

Fred is a brilliant student, but he does not like history.

a. Jenny works hard. She does not make good grades.
b. Our team has been defeated often. They persevere.
c. Great trials come to all of us. We must struggle against them.
d. So far Bill has had every good fortune. Expecting to be lucky, he only wastes time.
e. Todd does not take responsibility. He drifts aimlessly along.
f. You must have ambition. You will never succeed.
g. Unused talents are of little value. We should use our talents.
h. Most of us shun hard work. Success escapes us.
i. Conchita has a logical mind. She should become a lawyer.
j. Hank writes interesting stories. He is careless in his use of English.

422 VARIETY IN STRUCTURE PATTERNS Through variety in structure patterns, sentences may be kept free from monotony:

a. **Phrase** (390c): *Finishing the job,* the people left.
b. **Phrase** (390c): *Having finished the job,* the people left.
c. **Clause** (398): *The people who had finished the job* left.
d. **Clause** (408): *When the people finished the job,* they left.
e. **Absolute construction** (99): *The job being finished,* the people left.

f. **Absolute construction** (99): *The job finished,* the people left.
g. **Gerund** (56, 200): *After finishing the job,* the people left.

♦ The use of the participial phrase (390*c*) to replace the adjective clause (408) lends economy to and often strengthens the statement.

The person *standing beside the gate* is an officer. (**phrase**)
The person *who is standing beside the gate* is an officer. (**clause**)

Exercise 3.9   Phrases and Clauses.
The italicized group of words in each of the following sentences is either a phrase or a clause. On a separate sheet, rewrite each sentence, changing each italicized phrase to a clause and each italicized clause to a phrase.

EXAMPLE: *When we toured the museum,* we saw many art treasures.

Touring the museum, we saw many art treasures.

a. Joe has often told us *of his longing to travel through Asia.*
b. *Waiting for the others to come,* Elaine and I played table tennis.
c. *As they walked along Fifth Avenue,* they looked in all the windows.
d. The player *who is at bat now* is Dave Parker.
e. *The girls just coming to camp* are eager to see the new pool.
f. The old cottage *which overlooks the ocean* is falling apart.
g. *As I watched television intently,* I let my plate drop to the floor.
h. The author, *encouraged by the literary critics' praise,* started another novel.

423 **VARIETY IN ARRANGEMENT** In the arrangement of the material in sentences, there should be variety as to the place of emphasis. The periodic sentence (418) gives emphasis to the important idea in a sentence, but it should not be used either to the exclusion of the loose sentence (419) or, where appropriate, of the balanced sentence (420).

Yesterday afternoon about four o'clock my friend met with a serious accident. (**periodic sentence**)
My friend met with a serious accident yesterday afternoon about four o'clock. (**loose sentence**)

424 **VARIETY IN LENGTH** The length of sentences should be varied. Short sentences become tiresome when used to excess, and a sequence of long sentences has a tendency to make reading more difficult.

425 **VARIETY IN BEGINNING** Sentences which begin in the normal order (29) of subject first may become as tedious as any other oft-repeated sentence form; therefore, variety of beginning is important in gaining the reader's attention. The following beginnings suggest various ways of attaining variety.

426 A sentence may begin with a prepositional phrase (390*a*):

In those days people loved dangerous adventure.

427   A sentence may begin with a participial phrase (390*c*):

> *Hoping to reach home before the storm,* the rider urged his horse forward.
> *The day being clear,* we played tennis. (**absolute,** 99)

428   A sentence may begin with an adverb (316):

> *Silently and sadly* the old man turned away.

A sentence may begin with an adjective (275):

> *Beautiful* as the trees were, they were cut down for the new building.

429   A sentence may begin with a direct object of a verb (102):

> *Friends* and *enemies* alike he betrayed in order that he might gain wealth.

430   A sentence may begin with a dependent clause (398):

> *That you are in earnest* will help your cause. (**noun,** 400)
> *When the time comes,* we will act. (**adverb,** 409)

431   A sentence may begin with a verb (41) or verbal (198):

> *Work* hard if you wish to succeed.
> *To succeed* is the desire of nearly everyone. (**infinitive phrase,** 390*b*)
> *Helping others* gives real joy. (**gerund phrase,** 390*d*)

Exercise 3.10   Variety in Sentence Beginning.
For each of the following sentences, determine first whether it is a simple sentence, compound, complex, or compound-complex. Then identify the italicized beginning of each sentence as one of the following: verb, adverb, adjective, dependent clause, direct object, prepositional phrase, or participial phrase.

EXAMPLE: *Silently* the little boy slipped into the room.

> Simple   Adverb

a. *While Don and I were in Florida,* we had many interesting experiences; but we were happy to return home.
b. *Enchantingly* beautiful were many scenes which Don and I saw in Florida.
c. *In the Everglades* of Florida Don and I saw many unusual sights.
d. *Slender,* graceful evergreens are everywhere among the hills of Colorado.
e. *Beauty* of nature we behold each day as we stay here.
f. *Spend* a summer among the mountains if you enjoy the pleasures of nature.
g. *Thrilling to each new sight,* we really did find beauty in everything.
h. *Beside a lake* in a valley among the mountains stands a castle noted for its exotic beauty.
i. *Silently* we gazed upon the castle, which was noted for its exotic beauty.
j. *Standing in silence,* we gazed upon the Gothic castle.
k. *Slowly* we rowed the old boat, planning our trip for tomorrow.

l. *Great* plans we made as we rowed around the quiet lake.

m. *Making great plans for our trip,* we slowly rowed around the quiet lake.

n. *Great* satisfaction comes from the assurance of a task well done.

o. *That a task has been well done* brings real satisfaction.

p. *In the realization* of a task well done one finds great joy.

q. *Having finished a difficult task,* one feels great satisfaction.

r. *Work* we all do, but few of us do it thoroughly.

s. *Clearly* this is the better piece of work.

t. *Do* your work well if you would find satisfaction in achievement.

Effectiveness

432 EFFECTIVE SENTENCES An effective sentence must have **unity, coherence,** and **emphasis.**

433 **Unity** requires that the sentence must express connected thoughts; hence the relationship of thoughts must be clearly shown:

Weak: Fred Smith visited me last summer, and he once lived in England.
Better: Fred Smith, who visited me last summer, once lived in England.

434 **Coherence** requires that the connections between different parts of the sentence be made perfectly clear:

Confusing: Ruth returned the book which she had borrowed last week this afternoon.
Clear: This afternoon Ruth returned the book which she had borrowed last week.

435 **Emphasis,** or force, is given to the main ideas of a sentence by placing them properly in the position of greatest emphasis—the beginning and the close. Force is given by arranging ideas in order of climax, by repetition of words or sounds, by the use of figures of speech (630), by the addition of modifiers (275, 316), as well as by conciseness of expression and by variety (421-431):

a. Emphasis gained by **position:**
Poor: After a long search they found the lost child finally in the woods.
Better: After a long search in the woods they found the lost child.

b. Emphasis gained by **climax:**
Flood has brought to these people hunger, disease, death. (See **anticlimax,** 458)

c. Emphasis gained by **repetition:**
Mr. Smith is a man who is loyal—*loyal* to his friends, *loyal* to his family, *loyal* to his co-workers.

♦ The repetition of the same beginning letter or sound, called *alliteration,* is used effectively in advertising: *watch, wait, win.*

  d. Emphasis gained by **figures of speech**:
  Simile (631): The oak stood *like a sentinel.*
  Metaphor (632, 633): The rose is *queen* of all flowers.
  Personification (634): The trees *laughed* in the June sunlight.
  Hyperbole (635): He gave a *thousand* excuses for his failure.
  e. Emphasis gained by **addition of modifiers** (275, 316):
  He is a *handsome, intelligent, ambitious* young man.

436 A more **concise expression** sometimes adds force. Conciseness in statement may be gained by changes in form or style:

  a. An appositive (101) may be substituted for a sentence:

  Susan Smith addressed the meeting. *She is our president.*
  Susan Smith, *our president,* addressed the meeting.

  b. A participial phrase (394) may replace a clause (396)

  The man *who is standing near the desk* is the president.
  The man *standing near the desk* is the president.

  A participial phrase also may be used to replace a sentence:

  The beautiful building was destroyed by fire. *It was completed only a year ago.*
  The beautiful building, *completed only a year ago,* was destroyed by fire.

  c. A noun clause (400–407) may replace a sentence:
  Anita is ambitious. *That fact is self-evident.*
  That Anita is ambitious is self-evident.

  d. A gerund may make a sentence more concise (200, 266):

  It is my ambition to achieve a deserved success.
  Achieving a deserved success is my ambition.

  e. An infinitive may make a sentence more concise (199, 265):

  That I may win a deserved success is my ambition.
  To win a deserved success is my ambition.

Structure and Style

437 CONFUSING REFERENCES A sentence may be faulty because a pronoun is placed where it may refer to more than one word: There should be *no uncertainty* as to *what word* is *the antecedent* (129) of *a pronoun.*

438 Confusing reference of the relative pronoun:

  Confusing: She left the book on the table which she had just bought from the publisher. (The *which* seems to refer to *table,* though it should refer to *book.*)

Clear: She left on the table the book which she had just bought from the publisher. (The *which* clearly refers to *book*.)

439   Confusing reference of the personal pronoun:

Confusing: Harry told Fred that he would become a great musician. (It is not clear whether *he* refers to Harry or to Fred.)

Clear: Harry said to Fred, "You will become a great musician." OR, Harry said to Fred, "I will become a great musician."

440   An indefinite antecedent (129) of the pronoun:

Confusing: She asked me to help him, but I forgot about it. (The *it* has nothing definite to refer to.)

Clear: She made a request that I help him, but I forgot about it. (The antecedent is *request*.)

441   As a rule, avoid using *which* to refer to a clause (166, 376):

Ineffective: My uncle came to see me, which pleased me greatly.
Better: I was pleased because my uncle came to see me.

442   Do not misuse *them* for *those:*

I think those (not *them*) roses are lovely.

Do not use *they* with indefinite reference (169):

People (not *They*) say he is honest.

443   **UNRELATED IDEAS** Unrelated ideas should not be placed in the same sentence:

Disconnected: Fred won the race, and he likes chocolate candy.

444   **COMMA BLUNDER** (also **comma splice** or **fault**) Two independent clauses (397) should not be brought together only by a comma (except in the relatively rare cases where they make up a series, 496). They may, of course, be combined using a comma *and a conjunction.* Otherwise, they should be separated by a semicolon (489) or written as two sentences.

Incorrect: We spent the summer in Colorado, we had a good time.
Correct: We spent the summer in Colorado, and we had a good time.
Correct: We spent the summer in Colorado; we had a good time.
Correct: We spent the summer in Colorado. We had a good time.

445   **RUN-ON SENTENCES** A serious and common writing error is the run-on sentence in which two sentences are written as one without punctuation (35):

Incorrect: We rambled through the woods all day we did not reach home till late.
Correct: We rambled through the woods all day. We did not reach home till late.

♦ Related ideas may also, of course, be correctly expressed using a complex, compound, or compound-complex sentence form (421, 422).

446 **PERIOD FAULT** Through the misuse of the period, students sometimes write fragments for sentences:

Incorrect: We returned home. Hoping to have another picnic soon. (A participial phrase (390c) is written incorrectly as a sentence.)
Correct: We returned home, hoping to have another picnic soon.
Incorrect: They liked all kinds of games. Especially football.
Correct: They liked all kinds of games, especially football.
Incorrect: We had a good time. When we were in Colorado. (A dependent clause, 398, is written incorrectly as a sentence.)
Correct: We had a good time when we were in Colorado.

♦ Some professional writers occasionally do use the fragment very effectively in their work, but the beginning writer should construct complete sentences.

447 **AND-AND CONSTRUCTION** It sounds childlike to join many sentences by *and* as if all the ideas were of equal rank:

Childish: We finished our work, and we went fishing, and we had a good time.
Improved: After we had finished our work, we went fishing and had a good time.

448 **OMISSION OF NECESSARY WORDS** This common fault occurs in several ways:

   a. **Subject of sentence omitted.** The subject should be expressed in a declarative sentence (25) in order to make the meaning clear (33):

      Faulty: Went to the football game yesterday.
      Correct: I (*or* He, They, etc.) went to the football game yesterday.

♦ In the imperative sentence (26) the subject is correctly omitted:
Correct: Please lend me your book.

   b. **Subject of dependent clause omitted:**

      Not clear: When in Chicago, my father sent me a watch.
      Correct: When I was (*or* he was) in Chicago, my father sent me a watch.
      Not clear: When ten years old, his mother died.
      Correct: When he was ten years old, his mother died.

In elliptical sentences (5) the omission (ellipsis) of words gives strength rather than weakness, especially in the answers to questions.

Welcome. (*You are* welcome)
Where have I been? At school. (*I have been* at school.)
Do you like Shakespeare's plays? Yes. (Yes, *I like Shakespeare's plays.*)

449 PRIMER SENTENCES   Some students fall into the habit of writing monotonous short sentences like those in a primer:

Childish: We went to town. We stayed all day. We came home. We were tired.

Better: After we had spent the day in town, we came home tired.

♦ Short sentences may at times be used effectively, as an element of style, for emphasis.

She planned. She worked. She succeeded.

Exercise 3.11   Sentence Faults.

Each item in this exercise contains a comma blunder, a run-on blunder, a period fault, or ideas of unequal rank joined by a conjunction. Rewrite each item to improve it. Try to subordinate lesser ideas (433, 447) rather than write   primer sentences (449).

EXAMPLE: The speaker is here we can begin.

> *When the speaker is here, we can begin.*
>
> or
>
> *Because the speaker is here we can begin.*

a. Lynda has a scholarship, she expects to attend Harvard next year.
b. Our president has gone to the meeting he will bring us a report.
c. Helen is on our debating team and she likes to listen to radio forums.
d. Bob and I finished our work. While you and Jack were away.
e. Mary Jane is a friend to everyone, all the students like her.
f. Eric always does good work. Because he wants to go to college.
g. Betty won the race, and she is a good runner.
h. Charlotte attends law school, and she plays in a band, and she earns her expenses.
i. Tish likes biology she hopes to become a heart specialist.
j. We enjoyed the afternoon. Especially the drive in the park.
k. Roberta is a talented illustrator, and she is studying medieval art.
l. Everyone will have a good time. When we go on the picnic.
m. Ann writes poetry, and her brother is a reporter.
n. The boys are working hard. Hoping to complete the job soon.
o. Mary is the chairperson she will preside at the meeting.

450 PARALLEL STRUCTURE   Parallel thoughts should be expressed in terms that are grammatically parallel:

Faulty: *Swimming* is more enjoyable than *to row*. (One is a gerund and the other is an infinitive.)

Better: *Swimming* is more enjoyable than *rowing*. (Both are gerunds, 200).

Better: *To swim* is more enjoyable than *to row*. (Both are infinitives, 199.)

451 DANGLING MODIFIERS Modifiers should not be left dangling—with nothing to modify (271). A phrase (390c) or a prepositional phrase (390a) at the beginning of a sentence relates to the subject of that sentence. A participial phrase at the beginning of a sentence is followed by a comma:

> **Faulty:** Walking down the street, the beautiful building was admired. (The *building* did no *walking*.)
> **Clear:** Walking down the street, we admired the beautiful building.
> **Faulty:** On entering the room, the picture is seen. (There is nothing for the phrase to modify; the *picture* does not do the *entering*.)
> **Clear:** On entering the room, one may see the picture. (The introductory prepositional phrase which contains a gerund modifies *one*.)

452 MISPLACED MODIFIERS Modifiers—whether they are words (340), phrases, or clauses—should be so placed that their meaning is immediately clear to the reader (438):

> **Confusing:** She almost spent a hundred dollars.
> **Clear:** She spent *almost* a hundred dollars.
> **Confusing:** We saw a man on a horse with a wooden leg.
> **Clear:** We saw a *man with a wooden leg* on a horse.
> **Confusing:** Jane saw a hat in a window which she liked. (438)
> **Clear:** Jane *saw in a window* a hat which she liked.

Shifts in Structure

453 Avoid needless shifts in **person**:

> One must work if *one* (not *you*) would succeed.

454 Avoid needless shifts in **number**:

> A student should do *his* or *her* (not *their*) own work.

455 Avoid needless shifts in **voice** (254, 255):

> As we went up the path, *we saw a snake* (not *a snake was seen*).

456 Avoid needless shifts in **tense**:

> The hunter went into the woods, and there *he saw* (not *sees*) a deer.

457 Avoid needless shifts in **subject**:

> Ted's letters are interesting, because *they are cleverly written* (not *he is a clever boy*).

Exercise 3.12   Sentence Weaknesses.
Each item in this exercise contains a confusing reference of a pronoun; a dangling verbal modifier; a misplaced modifier; a needless shift in person, number,

or voice; or parallel thoughts not in parallel form. Rewrite each item, correcting the weaknesses.

EXAMPLE: Every boy should do their own work.

Every boy should do his own work.

a. Don told Jack that he had been invited to the party.
b. We campers like to swim and playing tennis.
c. When we went camping, a good time was had.
d. Ruth saw a leather coat in a shop window which she liked.
e. Working hard, the job was finally completed.
f. Marilyn told Louise that she would be appointed chairperson.
g. We saw some places in New Mexico which we liked.
h. Standing on the hill, the sunrise was colorful.
i. Each one of the girls should bring their swimming suit.
j. Overcoming odds is heroic, but to give up is cowardly.
k. Each girl should work hard if they hope to succeed.
l. Planning great things is easy, but to do them is difficult.
m. Opening the door, a strange sight was seen.
n. We went to the party and a wonderful time was had.
o. In the winter I like to skate and playing basketball.

Loss of Sentence Effectiveness

458 ANTICLIMAX   The sentence may lose effectiveness from anticlimax, the reverse of climax (435*b*), arranging ideas in the order of descending importance:

Flood has brought to these people *death, disease, hunger.*

459 EFFECTIVE REPETITION   Repetition of words may either strengthen or weaken a composition, depending upon whether important or trivial ideas are repeated.

460 A sentence may be strengthened by repetition of important words or ideas (435*c*)

461 MONOTONOUS REPETITION   Avoid the careless repetition of words:

Monotonous: *Autumn* is the most *enjoyable* time of year, because it is in *autumn* that the weather is most *enjoyable.*

Improved: *Autumn* is the most *enjoyable* time of the year, because it is the season when the weather is most pleasant.

462 WORDINESS   A sentence may lose some of its effectiveness through wordiness—lack of economy in the use of words:

Wordy: He spoke in a very enthusiastic manner to the boys and girls of the high school about the wonderful opportunities of the future which lay ahead of them.

Concise: He spoke with enthusiasm to the high-school students about the opportunities of the future.

Redundancy denotes the use of unnecessary words:

Joe, he works fast.   This here book is good.

Tautology is the needless repetition of an idea in different words:

Refer it back to me.   It is an ancient, old castle.

463 ARTIFICIAL EXPRESSION A sentence may lose in strength because of artificial expression:

Artificial: A vast concourse of those amicably inclined toward him assembled to do him honor on his natal day.
Natural: Many of his friends came to celebrate his birthday.

Exercise 3.13   Reviewing Sentence Weaknesses.
Each item in this lesson contains a defective sentence. The defects are caused by needless shifts in person or number or voice, by dangling verbal modifiers, by misplaced modifiers, by run-on blunders, by parallel thoughts not in parallel form, by incorrect uses of the comma or the period, or by confusing reference of a pronoun. Rewrite each item, making all changes necessary to correct sentence weaknesses.

EXAMPLE: Each boy must furnish their own ski equipment.

Each boy must furnish his own ski equipment.

a. Tom asked Dick if he thought he would be elected.
b. The new sweaters are here, have you seen them?
c. Rita thinks hiking is more fun than to bike.
d. Standing at the window, many people passed by.
e. Ellen has come have you seen her?
f. To fight for freedom is striving for the benefit of humanity.
g. The person who spoke was Gerald Myers he is our president.
h. Strolling through the woods, a waterfall was seen.
i. Hal Brown is our captain, do you know him?
j. Maria likes to write stories. Particularly historical stories.
k. We saw many things in the store which we wanted.
l. When we went fishing, many fish were caught.
m. Betsy and I stayed. Until the other women came.
n. If any boy wishes to take the course you must enroll now.
o. The coach likes to swim, he likes to skate, too.

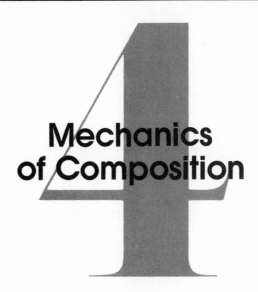

Mechanics of Composition

One meaning of the word *mechanics* is "Routine procedure: technical details or method." It has been a long time since the advent of printing gave impetus to the standardization of the "technical details" of the English language as we use it today. In so complicated a structure as language, change, of course, is always taking place. But tradition dies slowly, and the usage reported here represents the standards of *American English* for our time. We should not forget that other sectors of the English-speaking world—Great Britain, Canada, Australia, South Africa, the West Indies, for example—may have come to accept usage patterns that vary from that of American usage.

CAPITALIZATION

464 Every sentence except a short parenthetical sentence within another should begin with a capital letter:

> The day was beautiful.
> Mary left yesterday (she had been here a week) for New York.

465 In most English and American poetry written before the twentieth century each verse (line) begins with a capital letter:

> True ease in writing comes from Art, not Chance,
> As those move easiest who have learn'd to dance.—Alexander Pope

This convention is now disregarded by many contemporary poets.

466   The first word of a direct quotation in reported speech begins with a capital letter:

The girl said, "*W*ait for me."

467   The first word of a formal statement or resolution following introductory words (often italicized) is capitalized:

*Resolved, T*hat the world is growing better.

468   Every proper noun (55) (real or fictional) and every adjective derived from a proper noun (288) should be capitalized: *Boston, Bostonian; Spain, Spaniard; Samuel Johnson, Johnsonian; Miss Universe.*

469   The names of the days of the week, special holidays, and the names of the months are capitalized: *Sunday, Memorial Day, June.*

470   Names of the seasons are not capitalized ordinarily (483):

I like summer better than winter.

471   Names of particular associations and proper names resulting from membership in these associations are capitalized: *Republican Party, Republican; Democratic Party, Democrat; Methodist Church, Methodist; Garden Club; Vermont Historical Association.*

♦ Classes, schools, and colleges are capitalized when they refer to the particular:

John is a senior at Dickinson College, an excellent liberal arts college.
The Junior Class invited Joyce Carol Oates to speak.

472   Some abbreviations, such as the following, are written with capitals: A.D. (anno domini); B.C. (before Christ); SW (southwest); R.R. (railroad). Abbreviations of degrees and organizations are capitalized: A.B., M.D., Ph.D., A.A.A., A.C.S., U.S.A.

♦ A wide variation exists in the use of upper and lower case in abbreviations, as well as in the use of the period (487), which tends to be dropped in current usage.

473   Important historical events, documents, buildings, and monuments should be capitalized:

Battle of Hastings, World War II, the Declaration of Independence, The White House, Lincoln Memorial.

474   The words *east, west, north,* and *south* are capitalized when they mean particular sections of a country, but they are not capitalized when they mean direction.

He came from the *South.* (**a section of a country**)
He went *south* from town. (**a direction**)

The compounds of these words follow the same rule:

He lives in the great *Northwest.*
Is Hutchinson *northwest* of Wichita?

475 The names of deities, religions, sacred documents are capitalized: *Allah, Jehovah, Brahma, Zeus, Buddhism, Shintoism, the Koran, the Bible.*

476 Nouns and personal pronouns (132) referring to God or to Christ are capitalized; but some writers do not capitalize the personal pronoun when its antecedent (129) is expressed:

I know *He* is the Lord.   Jesus loves *his* friends.

477 Names for the Bible and its parts and books begin with capital letters:

Bible, the Scriptures, Old Testament, Deuteronomy. (Do not italicize such words in running text.)

478 The first, last, and important words in the titles of books, literary articles, pictures, musical compositions, chapters of books, poems, plays, stories, newspapers, and magazines begin with capitals. Prepositions, articles, and conjunctions are usually not capitalized unless they begin the title, but prepositions of five or more letters may be capitalized; a preposition at the end of a title is capitalized. If an article begins the official title of a magazine or newspaper, it should be capitalized:

"Ode on a Grecian Urn"   He reads *The New York Times.*

479 The pronoun *I* and the vocative *O* (O Apollo) are always capitalized, but the interjection *oh* is capitalized only when it begins a sentence or stands alone:

Oh, will they come?   *Oh!*

480 The initials of a person's name are capitalized.

481 Titles used with proper names are capitalized:

We think that *Captain Smith* would make a good leader.
He saw *Principal John Moore* at the meeting.

482 When a civil or personal title is used as a proper noun referring to a specific person or thing, it is correct to capitalize it.

Ann went with *Mother* and me to see her mother and father.
Will you help me, *Father,* with my work?
The *Secretary of State* will be named soon.
Our *Federal Government* differs from other federal governments.

483 Common nouns are capitalized when they are strongly personified:

Come, lovely *Spring,* and make us glad.

484 A common noun, such as *river, mountain, park, lake, gulf, ocean, street, avenue, hotel, church, school, club, society,* or *company,* is properly capitalized when it becomes a part of a particular name:

Is Lowell *School* near Belmont *Park?*
Does Clifton *Avenue* cross Maple *Street?*

Newspaper usage, although not all mass media follow it, shows some variation of this rule as in these examples:

Is Lowell school near Belmont park?
Does Clifton avenue cross Maple street?

But when the common noun precedes the particular name, it is capitalized even in the newspapers:

He lives near *Lake* Erie.

485 It is good practice to refer to a good dictionary for the capitalization of words as proper nouns and adjectives. Many words do have correct usage as both common (generic) and proper nouns: *renaissance-Renaissance, revolution-Revolution, ohm-Ohm, watt-Watt.*

Exercise 4.1   Capitalization.
Rewrite the following sentences, correcting capitalization where necessary.

EXAMPLE: Did ~~W~~ill ~~J~~ames write ~~S~~moky?

a. One memorial day my Friend, mary jo grant, went with us to flint, michigan.
b. Two noted Writers of the fifties are j. d. salinger and r. w. ellison.
c. The farewell address by president washington and the constitution of the united states are required reading in blair school.
d. My Father went with uncle sam to yom kippur services at temple torah yesterday.
e. On friday the Orchestra of lake junior high school will play the *rosamunde overture.*
f. My Sister, ms. clare ash, studied last fall at hood college, frederick, maryland.
g. When did the battle of bunker hill take place?
h. My father gave mother a fine color print of the painting "the ballet class" by Dégas.
i. Last wednesday mr. frye, talking about thanksgiving day in new england, quoted from the bible.
j. Mother is a republican, father a democrat.

PUNCTUATION

Period

486 A period should be placed at the end of every declarative (25) and every imperative (26) sentence unless it is used as an exclamatory (28) sentence or in a sentence used parenthetically within another sentence (464). An elliptical expression (5, 448) used as a substitute for a sentence is followed by a period or other end punctuation:

> Jean went to Europe last summer. **(declarative)**
> Let me see your new book. **(imperative)**
> Annette Jones (she is president of our class) will preside. **(parenthetical sentence** with no capital, 464, and no period) Yes. **(elliptical)**

♦ The polite request expressed in interrogative form so frequent in letters is generally followed by a period, not a question mark (529):

> Will you please send your latest catalog.

487 Use periods after a person's initials and some abbreviations (538):

> Geo. F. Smith; A.D.; B.C.; A.M.; Mr.; Mrs.; Ms.

There are many exceptions, such as *IQ, DDT*. Abbreviations of many organization names omit periods: *WAFS, WAVES*—especially if they may be pronounced as a word (an acronym)—or they may be written either way:

> *Y.M.C.A.* or *YMCA, USMC* or *U.S.M.C.*

Consult the dictionary as a guide to the handling of abbreviations. Do not use a period after a contraction or after a shortened form of a name used as a part of a whole name:

> *Ben* Brown *isn't* here.

Only one period is necessary at the end of a sentence even when it ends with an abbreviation, but a question mark (529) may follow the period used after an abbreviation at the end of a sentence:

> A great battle was fought in the year 490 B.C.
> What battle was fought in the year 490 B.C.? (Marathon)
> What great siege occurred in A.D. 490? (Ravenna)

488 Three periods are used to form an *ellipsis*, which indicates an omission in quoted material:

> "He did his best . . . yet he never quite succeeded."

A fourth period is used at the end of a sentence.

Four periods show that a whole sentence (or sentences) has been omitted:

> "He said they would come . . . . But they never did come."

The period is used between the integral and decimal parts of a mixed fraction and between figures indicating dollars and cents:

The lake is 62.35 miles long. One mile is 1.609 kilometers.
With the discount it will cost $14.22.

Semicolon

489   Use a semicolon between two clauses of a compound sentence (415) when they are not joined by a conjunction (365–369), unless they are very short and are used informally (496).

The rain fell in torrents; we turned everywhere for shelter. (This may be also stated as two sentences.)
He came, he saw, he went away.

490   The semicolon is used between clauses of a compound sentence which are joined by conjunctive adverbs (320), such as *therefore, hence, however, nevertheless, accordingly, thus, then:*

The day was very cold; therefore, we did not go for a ride.

491   The semicolon is properly used between clauses which are joined by conjunctions if the clauses are long, or when the clauses have internal commas:

John arrived last night, I am told; but because his plane was late, he could not come to the party.

492   The semicolon is often used to prevent misreading:

We invited Cindy Webb, the captain of the team; Don Mills, the president of our class; and Joe Wynn, the chairperson of our group.

Colon

493   The colon is used to introduce formally a word, a list, examples, a statement or question, a series of statements, or a long quotation. An expression such as *the following* often precedes the list:

The following fruits are for sale: apples, peaches, pears.

494   A colon is used after the salutation of a business letter and is used between the parts of a number denoting time:

Dear Sir or Madam: The plane arrives at 6:15 A.M.

Comma

495   The general rule is that a comma is used between the clauses of a compound sentence (415) when they are joined by such conjunctions as *but, for, or, and.* Use the comma with *but* (unless the subject is the same); use the comma with *for* (and when needed to show it is not a preposition); use the comma with *or* (when the subject shifts); use the comma with *and* (unless the subject is closely connected in thought). If, however, the clauses are long or have commas within them, a semicolon should be used to separate them (see 491).

> Robert entered the race, but he did not win.
> Robert entered the race but did not win.
> Robert sent them a letter, for he had to know.
> Robert told them where to look, for he knew.
> Robert was happy or he thought he was.
> Robert was happy, or we would not have found him.
> Robert dressed carefully, and on the way out he spoke to his father.
> Robert dressed carefully and he wore his best suit.

496 Very short clauses making up a series and not joined by conjunctions may be separated by commas (489, 504):

> She came, she looked, she went away.

497 An adverbial clause (409) which precedes a main clause (397), unless it is very short, is set off by a comma:

> When my cousin came to spend the day with me, she found me at work.
> If you expect to succeed, you must prepare yourself.

The comma is usually omitted when the adverbial clause follows the main clause.

> My cousin found me at work when she came to spend the day with me.

498 A comma should be used to set off *yes* or *no* used as mild interjections or as sentence adverbs:

> Yes, you may go.

Other mild interjections (46), such as *ah, oh, well, why,* are set off by commas when exclamation marks would be too strong:

> Ah, well, who can tell what may happen?

499 Nonrestrictive phrases and clauses should be set off from the rest of the sentence by a comma or commas. A nonrestrictive phrase or clause is a nonessential phrase or clause; that is, it is a phrase or a clause which can be omitted without changing the meaning of the main clause (sentences *b, c,* and *f* have a restrictive or limiting clause or phrase):

> a. Edgar Allan Poe, who wrote "The Raven," was an American writer. (The clause *who wrote "The Raven"* is not necessary to the meaning of the main clause.)
> b. Students who study will learn. (The clause *who study* is necessary to explain which students will learn.)
> c. The girl who sells the tickets is an honor student. (*Who sells the tickets* is necessary to explain which girl is an honor student.)
> d. Jane Gray, *who sells the concert tickets,* is a member of our class. (The

clause is not necessary; it merely explains that the girl sells tickets.)

  e. The boy, *seeing the clouds,* hurried home. (The phrase is not necessary to explain *boy*.)

  f. The girl *holding the flag* is Margaret. (The phrase is necessary to tell which girl is Margaret.)

  g. *Wishing to see the parade,* we went to town early. (A participial phrase, 390c, that stands at the beginning of a sentence is followed by a comma.)

  h. *The task being done,* we went home. (absolute construction, 99)

Restrictive or limiting clauses or phrases are not set apart by punctuation.

Exercise 4.2   Punctuating Clauses.

Copy the following sentences, underlining any restrictive clauses and setting off the nonrestrictive clauses with commas.

EXAMPLE: I read the story <u>that Ted wrote.</u>

Bob's father, who works on the night shift, is trying to sleep.

a. Our principal who was educated in Europe is a very good speaker.
b. The President who is most interesting to me is Abraham Lincoln.
c. For driving in the desert one needs a car that is air-conditioned.
d. My father works in a factory that makes oil-well equipment.
e. Jack doesn't like tennis which is my favorite sport.
f. Ginger which is a very old and favorite spice is also of value in medicine.
g. The Italian artist who painted this picture is world-renowned.
h. My brother Joe who claims not to like music enjoyed the symphony concert.
i. Shoes that fit properly are essential for a good appearance.
j. I don't like speakers who ramble.
k. Last night's speaker who knew her subject well had no difficulty at all in holding our attention.
l. We had a talk by Ed's sister who is a civil engineer.
m. We must not elect a mayor who can't manage the city's affairs efficiently.
n. Color film that is made for indoor use may be used outdoors by using a filter.
o. Emerson who is famous as an essayist and poet was also a very popular lecturer.
p. I think *Macbeth* which is a tragedy is Shakespeare's best play.
q. Our dog which is a Scottish Terrier always wants to chase cats.
r. I want a small dog that I can train.
s. I have a wristwatch which runs underwater.
t. The court house which was built twenty years ago is now inadequate.

500 Items of a parenthetical nature are set off by commas. Two commas are necessary when the expression is within the sentence and no other mark is used.

Such items include persons addressed, appositives, items in addresses and dates, as well as independent phrases and clauses:

Will you help me, *Harry,* with this work?
Nan Gray, *my favorite cousin,* is here.
Tom came from Dallas, *Texas,* yesterday.
Jane was born on June 12, *1952,* in Seattle.
That boy is, *I believe,* a dependable fellow.

When an appositive (101) is an attribute or part of the proper name, or is closely connected with the word it explains, no comma is used:

Edward *the Confessor* was there.
My cousin *Nell* lives in Arizona.

501 A direct quotation equivalent to a sentence should be separated from explanatory matter by a comma or commas. But a sentence quoted within another sentence may be so closely connected with the rest of the sentence that no comma is needed:

The girl said, "Wait for me."
"Wait for me," the girl said.
"Wait," the girl said, "until I come."
Her cheerful greeting was always "How do you do today?"

No comma is used before an indirect quotation or a title in quotation marks unless there is a special need for it:

Fred said that he went to Chicago.
Longfellow wrote "The Psalm of Life."

502 Items in a date are set off by commas:

They were married on Saturday, June 26, 1965. (or 26 June 1965)

In a date consisting of month and year only, commas are usually omitted:

In August 1965 we were on vacation. (or August, 1965)

503 Use commas for explanatory matter in connection with a direct quotation, unless stronger punctuation is necessary (495):

"It's time," she said, "for me to go home."
"It is time to go," she said; "it is very late."

504 Use commas to separate the items of a series of words, phrases, or short clauses:

The farmer sold corn, hay, oats, potatoes, and wheat.
They come from the east, from the west, from the north, and from the south.
He rose, he smiled, he began to speak.

505 A series of adjectives of the same rank modifying the same noun are separated by commas unless they are joined by conjunctions. No comma is used after the last adjective:

We saw tall, slender, graceful trees.
He drew the trees as tall, slender, and graceful.
A steep and narrow path led on.

When the adjective next to the noun seems to be a part of the noun, no comma is used before it:

He is a courteous young man. (*Courteous* modifies *young man*.)

506 A comma may sometimes be necessary for clarity of meaning:

Ever since, Frank has been a better boy.
You would, would you?

Exercise 4.3   Capitalization and Punctuation.
Copy the following sentences, crossing out each incorrect lower-case letter and writing the capital above it. Insert punctuation marks where they are needed.

$$S \quad B$$
EXAMPLE: Let's read "The spectre bridegroom."

a. Most students have read *The sketch book* by Washington Irving.
b. This gifted author was born in New york City on april 3 1783.
c. When he was a boy he often walked along the banks of the hudson river near Tarrytown and talked to the country folk.
d. He was the first of our writers to become famous in europe and he was our first american literary diplomat.
e. Because he had an excellent sense of humor irving wrote amusing stories.
f. His "Rip Van winkle and The legend of sleepy hollow" deal with old dutch legends of the Hudson River Valley.
g. Such delightful characters as ichabod crane and rip van winkle appeal to us all.
h. Irving delighted in telling of such events as the party at the van tassel home.
i. In another story The spectre bridegroom, he recounts another old dutch country legend.
j. Several of irving's stories tell of the american indians of his time.
k. Other stories of his give accounts of christmas customs in england.
l. In *The Sketch Book* he tells of the home of William shakespeare westminster abbey and the cathedral of london.
m. When he was on the staff of the american Legation in madrid spain he was invited to live in the Alhambra by the king.
n. He finished his famous *life of Washington* a fine work when he was seventy-six.
o. In 1842 he was appointed united states Minister to spain.

   p. At the time he was writing american writers had won little recognition in europe.

   q. He is one of our most entertaining authors his stories are delightfully told.

   r. Most of us like to recall ichabod crane as he rides forth on gunpowder to attend katrina's party.

   s. With pleasure we recall ichabod's thrilling race with the headless horseman.

   t. Also, we like to wander with rip van winkle into the vastnesses of the catskill mountains.

Quotation Marks

507 Quotation marks are used to enclose a direct quotation. They are not used with indirect quotations:

   "You are to blame," she said.
   He said *that he would go home.*

508 Quotation marks or italics are used to distinguish words or letters referred to merely as words or letters. (Italics are preferred in printed form for this use.)

   You may parse the words "they" and the two "a's" in that sentence.

◆ Avoid using quotation marks where they are not required by the rules of composition mechanics. Do not use quotation marks for simple emphasis or for adornment.

509 Quotation marks are used with: the titles of articles; the chapter titles of books; the titles of short poems, songs, and stories; and the parts of a musical composition. (Italics are used in print for titles of books; periodicals; names of ships, airplanes, satellites, spacecraft, etc., 539.)

   He read Whittier's "Maud Muller."
   The article was called "Capturing the Imagination."
   I have read Hawthorne's "Rappaccini's Daughter."
   He listened to the "Third Movement" of the *Ninth Symphony.*

◆ One line drawn under a handwritten or typed word indicates that it would be italicized in print.

510 A long quotation of several paragraphs may have quotation marks at the beginning of each paragraph and at the end of the last paragraph. However, most long quotations are set off by additional indention or by smaller type or by both, and in this case no quotation marks are used in print. (See examples in 544 and 545.)

511 In reporting conversation, each speech or fragment of speech (515)—no matter how short—should be in quotation marks. An uninterrupted quotation in one paragraph, though long, should have but one set of quotation marks (beginning and ending):

"Do you know me?" he asked.
"I am not sure," she replied, "that I have ever met you."
"I am your old schoolmate, Edgar Jones," he explained.

512 Nicknames and words or phrases used ironically may be put in quotations:

My friend "T-Bone" was at the picnic.
His "limousine" was a jalopy. (Be sparing of this use; it may become very annoying.)

♦   Usually quotation marks are omitted from nicknames after the first use or when the nickname (such as *Babe* Ruth) is well known. Many writers also use quotation marks to distinguish technical terms and words used in very specialized meaning.

Often it is better to avoid the use of slang and faulty diction than to apologize for it with quotation marks. Whenever the slang phrase is too expressive to admit of a more prosaic substitution, assume responsibility for using it instead of quoting it.

513 A quotation within a quotation should be enclosed in single quotation marks, and a quotation within that should be in double marks:

"I was surprised," Mary admitted, "when he said, 'I agree with Shakespeare, "All the world's a stage." ' "

514 A question mark or an exclamation mark is placed inside the quotation mark if it is a part of the quotation; outside, if it applies to the main clause. The period or the comma is always placed before the quotation mark (note example in 513); the colon or semicolon is placed outside:

"Are you ill?" she asked.
Did Father say, "Wait until tomorrow"?
Tom said, "Don't wait for me"; then he turned and walked away.
"The music was beautiful," she remarked.

If both the main clause of the sentence and the quotation are interrogative, only one question mark (529) is required:

Did Fred ask, "Where have you been?"

515 When a quotation is interrupted, an extra set of marks must be used:

"Come," he said, "as soon as you have the time."

516 There is often an erroneous impression among students that all interruptions of quotations are marked by commas. Use the sentence marks which should be used regardless of the quotation:

"You have delayed too long already," he said. "Success comes to people who act."

"I am sure!" she exclaimed; "there is no doubt about it."

Apostrophe

517   Use the apostrophe to indicate the omission of letters from words. It should be placed immediately above the point of omission:

The man *isn't* here.

♦ Do not confuse: *its* for *it's*, or *your* for *you're*.

518   The apostrophe may be used with *s* to denote plurals of letters, figures, signs, symbols, and words considered merely as words (88):

She used two *a's*, three *b's*, two *8's* (or *8s*), two *and's* (or *ands*).

519   The apostrophe is used in forming the possessive of nouns and indefinite pronouns. To form the possessive singular, add the apostrophe and s (120):

The *bird's* plumage is brilliant.
He is *everyone's* friend.

To form the possessive plural of a noun whose plural ends in s, add an apostrophe only (121):

Boys' suits are on sale.

♦ Some words admit of two forms (120):

Burns' or *Burns's, James'* or *James's.*   (The second form seems preferred.)

520   The possessives of the personal pronouns such as *its, his, hers, ours, yours,* and *theirs* (146) do not use the apostrophe. But indefinite pronouns, such as *either, one,* and *other,* do use the apostrophe:

The cat wants *its* (not *it's*) dinner. (*Its* is **possessive.**)
It's time to go home. (*It's* is a **contraction,** 146, 517.)
One must do *one's* duty, but always respect the *other's* rights.

521   The apostrophe is omitted from proper names in cases where a proper noun is used as a proper adjective, a standard English usage (some geographic names, organization or company names, etc.):

Pikes Peak, Citizens National Bank, Teachers College.

Dash

522   A dash is used to mark a sudden change or break in a sentence:

The boy went there—where did he go?
"There is no—" The speaker could not go on. (No period is needed after a dash which breaks off a sentence.)
Smith told me—but don't mention this—that he was bankrupt.

523   The dash may be used to set off a parenthetic group, especially when the parenthetic expression contains commas:

His food—nuts, berries, small game—was adequate for survival.

524   The dash may be used before a summarizing statement:

He planned, he worked, he sacrificed—all these he did that he might succeed.

525   The dash may be used to lend emphasis:

For a thousand dollars—a mere thousand dollars—he betrayed his friend.

♦ A double-length dash may be used to indicate the omission of letters or words:

Have you seen Captain H—— lately?   No, but I have seen——.

Parentheses and Brackets

526   Parentheses may be used to enclose matter apart from the main thought:

If you come to see me (and I hope you do come), be sure to bring your camera.

Matter enclosed in parentheses within a sentence, even though it forms a complete declarative or imperative sentence, need not begin with a capital and need not end with a period. But if it is interrogative or exclamatory, it ends with the appropriate mark (529, 530, 531):

She says that you insulted her (did you?) and that she was furious.

527   The punctuation mark belonging to matter given before that set off by parentheses should be placed after the second parenthesis mark (see the first example sentence given in 526):

When you receive your appointment (and I hope you receive it soon), you must tell me of your plans.

When a complete, independent sentence is placed in parentheses, the final punctuation is placed inside the parentheses:

(These stories will be further explained in the next chapter.)

528   Brackets are used to enclose explanatory matter that one inserts in a quotation from another writer:

According to the novelist Walker Percy, "[Robert E.] Lee was the nearest thing we [the South] had to a saint—and it is no accident that our saint was a general."

Brackets are also used to enclose parenthetical material occurring inside a unit already enclosed within parentheses:

"Go west, young man" (often attributed incorrectly to Horace Greeley [editor of *The New York Tribune*]) was actually written first by John Babsone Lane Soule.

Question Mark

529 Place a question mark after every direct question. Although the very short declarative sentence (25) within parentheses (486) does not require a period, the short interrogative sentence (27) so used must close with a question mark (526):

Have you seen my new hat?

When you come to see me (why not come soon?), I will tell you about my trip to Denver.

If the main clause of a sentence and the dependent clause are both interrogative (27), only one question mark (514) is used. No question mark is used after an indirect question. After a polite request a period should be used instead of a question mark:

Did the coach ask, "When did you return?"
He inquired what the trouble was.
Will you please send the check at once.

530 A question mark within parentheses is used to express uncertainty about dates or other information:

Lucretius, 96(?)–55 B.C.

In sentences it is usually better to use *about* or *probably* than to use the question mark; in this case: Lucretius was born *about* 96 B.C.

Exclamation Mark

531 The exclamation mark is used after words, expressions, or sentences to show strong feeling or forceful utterance:

Fire! Fire!   How terrible it was!

An exclamation within parentheses (526) retains the exclamation mark:

She left the door unlocked (how thoughtless!) and drove to the store.

Exercise 4.4   Punctuation and Capitalization.
Rewrite the following sentences, correcting punctuation and capitalization where necessary. Circle the changes you make.

EXAMPLE: The Speaker quoted from Shooting script a poem by Adrienne Rich.

The ⓢpeaker quoted from ⓒShooting ⓢcript⊙ⓒa poem by Adrienne Rich.

a. Ed alice and Bob are students at Ohio university not Ohio state.
b. Hank is I believe a hard working clever senior he deserves the award.
c. Did you hear Eric say we must leave soon
d. Last Summer we visited baltimore maryland
e. My Mother said if you want to go you should pack now
f. that farmer raises corn rye oats and barley however wheat is his principal crop.
g. Margaret Mitchell who wrote gone with the wind lived in the south.
h. Twenty six students from Wade high school are trying for the scholarship.
i. Mr. Black lives north of kansas city however he works in St Joseph

HYPHENATION

532   A hyphen should be used to join words combined into a single adjective modifier: *well-to-do, self-supporting, far-flung.*

Adverbs ending in *ly* do not change into hyphenated compound modifiers: a *beautifully illustrated* story.

533   The hyphen is omitted when certain compound modifiers follow the word modified and a linking verb, but true compounds retain the hyphen in this position:

His mother is self-supporting.   His mother is well liked.

Use your dictionary as a guide to the correct usage of compounds.

534   Hyphens are used in spelling compound numbers from twenty-one to ninety-nine.

535   Fractions are hyphenated only when used as modifiers:

One half of the book is finished. **(noun)**
The box is two-thirds full. **(adverb)**
He won by a two-thirds majority. **(adjective)**

536   A **compound word** is one that is made up of two or more words joined together either with or without a hyphen. The purpose of a compound is to express an idea that the component parts do not express separately either in meaning or in grammatical function. They may be called *hyphemes* or *solidemes.* A purpose of the hyphen is also to avoid letter combinations that confuse the reader and to make a visual distinction for proper word stress. Examples:

   a. red coat (garment); *b. redcoat* (soldier); *c. red-coated* (covered with red).

A good dictionary is the best guide to the correct form to use: two-word compound, solideme, or hypheme.

537   When it is necessary to divide a word at the end of a line, the division should be made between syllables, and a hyphen should be placed at the end of the line. Never place a hyphen at the beginning of a line. Always check the dictionary for correct syllabication of English words.

ABBREVIATIONS AND CONTRACTIONS

538   The following rules should be observed in using abbreviations and contractions (see also 487):

   a.   The use of many abbreviations in formal writing indicates carelessness on the part of the writer. However, there are a few abbreviations which are used regularly in formal writing: A.B., B.C., A.M., P.M., (when used with figures); Mr., Mrs., Ms., Dr. (when used with names).

   b.   It is considered impolite to abbreviate titles such as the following when used before the last name only: *captain, general, colonel, professor, president.*

   c.   The old rule was to place a period after each abbreviation, but there are a growing number of exceptions to the rule (see 487).

   Contractions and Roman numerals used in sentences do not require periods after them:

   He doesn't live here.   James II was king of England.

   Periods are not used with scientific or technical symbols: H_2SO_4, sin, tan, cos.

   Always refer to the dictionary for unfamiliar forms.

ITALICS (UNDERLINING)

539   The following rules should be observed in using italics:

   a.   In writing in longhand and in typing, place one line under a word to indicate that it should be printed in italics.

   b.   Italicize foreign terms which have not become anglicized. The dictionary is the only safe guide in determining these words.

   c.   Italicize a word, phrase, or letter used as a subject of discussion (see also 508):

   The word *receive* is often misspelled.

   d.   Use italics (see *a*.) to indicate the titles of books, magazines, newspapers, and the names of ships, named trains, aircraft, and man-made spacecraft:

We have just read *The Sea Around Us* by Rachel L. Carson and an article, "Pollution of the Air," in *Harper's*.

On 20 February 1962 John H. Glenn, Jr., made three orbits of the earth in *Friendship 7*. *Apollo 15,* with astronauts Scott, Irvin, and Worden, began its famous trip to the moon on 26 July 1971.

e. It is permissible to italicize a word for emphasis, but this use of italics should be rare:

He *would* go back in spite of everything.

NUMERALS

540 The following rules should be observed in writing numerals:

a. Dates, street numbers, page numbers, decimals, and percents should be written in figures:

Columbus reached the New World on *October 12, 1492.*
Tom lives at *16* Spruce Street.   His address is listed on page *16.*
Jim got *60* percent of the vote for class president.

b. The sign $ is not used for a sum less than one dollar:

The knife cost *sixty-five cents.*

c. The general rule for writing numbers is to spell out the number if it may be done in one or two words; otherwise, it should be written in figures:

He gave me *one thousand* dollars.
He gave me *1397* copies of the paper; there were *10,491* printed.

d. When several numbers (used as statistics) are mentioned within a short space of text, use figures for all.

e. A number which represents a person's age or one denoting the hour of the day is usually spelled out:

At *three o'clock* there is to be a meeting of the students who are between *sixteen* and *eighteen* years of age.

f. Do not begin a sentence with figures:

Six hundred twenty-five (not 625) students were at the meeting.

g. It is not necessary, except in special instances such as contracts or laws, to place numerals in parentheses after written numbers; but when they are used, each should follow the number it repeats:

I am sending you *fifteen (15) bushels* of wheat.

h. In technical, mathematical, and business writing, figures are generally used:

125 square feet, *$6.00* a pound, *4½* percent, *9.6* meters.

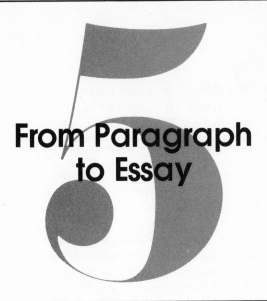

From Paragraph to Essay

Think of the house you live in as if it were a composition. Everything about your house has a specific name and function—the words of language. Each window or door, every wall or roof, is related to the whole—words in proper combination become the sentence. Each room, with its doors, windows, walls, ceiling, and furniture, becomes a unit of the whole—the sentences in logical sequence become the paragraph. Your house is made up of a series of rooms (unless it is a one-room house!)—the paragraphs in their turn become a composition. Compositions, like the houses people live in, have many styles: essay, story, letter, news report, speech, research paper, sermon, poem, novel, play, review, précis.

STRUCTURE AND ANALYSIS

541 **WHAT IS A PARAGRAPH?** The paragraph is usually described as a group of sentences developing a single topic. Sometimes a paragraph may consist of a single topic sentence; at other times, several paragraphs may be needed to develop a topic.

542 **LENGTH OF THE PARAGRAPH** The length of the paragraph in general writing is determined primarily by the extent to which the ideas are developed. This rule, however, is not arbitrary and may be modified, as for instance in the business letter (608), in which the short paragraph is more effective than the longer one. In dialogue, of course, each speech is separately paragraphed as a rule.

543 **PARAGRAPH SENSE** Every good writer develops a paragraph sense, just as he develops a sentence sense (36). This sense may be acquired by thinking in terms of topics and by adhering strictly to each topic under discussion.

544 **TOPIC SENTENCE** The sentence that presents the topic to be discussed is called the **topic sentence**. It is often stated at the beginning of the paragraph—but it may occur at any point in a paragraph—and its position may be varied to avoid monotony. The following paragraph illustrates the beginning topic sentence:

> The *McGuffey Eclectic Readers* are of more value to us today as cultural artifacts than as educational textbooks. In many respects they offer a fascinating survey of American nineteenth-century life and values (with a few curious historical omissions, such as the glamour of the river steamboats and the California gold rush). But their legacy is much more significant than this, even if harder to measure. Wielding an influence second only to the Bible over millions of minds, they played a major role in establishing the moral, social, and literary values of several generations. In so doing, the *McGuffey Readers* served as a primary force in shaping the present consciousness of what we now call Middle America.

♦ Sometimes no single sentence will express the topic of the paragraph. Except for transition paragraphs, however, the paragraph's primary purpose should be identifiable.

545 **DEVELOPING THE TOPIC** There are many ways of developing the topic, some of the most common being the use of *details, examples, comparison* or *contrast, cause and effect,* or a combination of any two or more of these methods. An illustration is given for each of the first three:

   a. **Details**. Giving details makes a topic more vivid and develops at greater length what is suggested in the topic. Here is a familiar paragraph from "The Legend of Sleepy Hollow," by Washington Irving.

> All was now bustle and hubbub in the late quiet schoolroom. The scholars were hurried through their lessons, without stopping at trifles; those who were nimble skipped over half with impunity, and those who were tardy had a smart application now and then in the rear, to quicken their speed, or help them over a tall word. Books were flung aside without being put away on the shelves, inkstands were overturned, benches thrown down, and the whole school was turned loose an hour before the usual time, bursting forth like a legion of young imps, yelping and racketing about the green, in joy of their early emancipation.

   b. **Examples**. Concrete examples are given to illustrate the general suggestion of the topic:

Riverside Park is noted for the beauty and variety of its native trees. Along the river to the south are many excellent specimens of elm, sycamore, cottonwood, and hackberry. To the west, covering several acres, is a grove of tall, beautiful black walnut trees, shading here and there a less stately mulberry. To the north the park abounds in large shapely oaks, some of which thrust out protecting arms above clumps of timid redbuds. Other less prominent specimens scattered throughout the park are ash, box elder, and Osage orange.

c. **Contrast.** Through contrast, differences are made to stand out more prominently. Notice the effect of this method in the paragraph below, from "The Country Church," by Washington Irving:

As I have brought these families into contrast, I must notice their behavior in church. That of the nobleman's family was quiet, serious, and attentive. Not that they appeared to have any fervor of devotion, but rather a respect for sacred things, and sacred places, inseparable from good breeding. The others, on the contrary, were in a perpetual flutter and whisper; they betrayed a continual consciousness of finery, and the sorry ambition of being the wonders of a rural congregation.

In developing a topic explaining a process, such as building something, follow its normal order. The construction of an article would be described by the selection of the materials on through the different stages in a step-by-step sequence.

546 MECHANICS OF WRITING PARAGRAPHS

a. Indent the first line of each paragraph. In longhand, it is customary to indent about an inch; in typing, the usual indentation is five or ten spaces.
b. Do not leave a part of a line blank except at the close of the paragraph.
c. Except when the length of the paragraph is arbitrary, as it is in dialogue, it should seldom be made either extremely long or short.
d. In dialogue, begin a paragraph with each change of speaker.
e. Keep the left margin of the paragraph uniform and the right margin reasonably so. Paragraph indention should be uniform.
f. Make the transition from paragraph to paragraph easy and natural, sometimes by the use of appropriate transition words (549), but always by proper arrangement.

♦ Some business firms do not indent typewritten paragraphs in their letters. This style is called **flush-paragraphing** or **block style**. Sometimes, too, printers begin paragraphs at the margin as an element of the typographic design.

PARAGRAPH REQUIREMENTS

547 The paragraph, like the sentence (433–435), must have **unity, coherence**, and **emphasis**.

548 **Unity in the paragraph** is attained when every sentence bears directly upon the topic of that particular paragraph. Any departure from the central topic means that a new paragraph should be formed. In the following paragraph the italicized sentence is irrelevant and therefore should be eliminated:

> You will find in this car all the qualities you desire most in a motor car—economy, style, comfort, efficiency, endurance. With its low first cost and inexpensive operation it has long been the acknowledged economy leader. It is also a style leader, and it offers every modern comfort expected in even the most expensive type of car. *Owners are enthusiastic about it because of its easy steering.* In speed and safety and sureness of high performance it defies competition. Year after year it continues to give superior service unhampered by the inconvenience and expense of repair.

Exercise 5.1   Paragraph Unity.

The two numbered sentences below could serve as topic sentences for paragraphs. Under each topic sentence are sentences giving details such as might be noted in preparing a paper on the subject. List which of the lettered sentences should *not* be included in the paragraphs.

1. **The peacetime duties of our Coast Guard involve varied and dangerous activities.**

   a. Its life-saving stations are ready in all kinds of weather for search and rescue missions at sea.
   b. Its rescue service is provided for any person or ship regardless of nationality.
   c. The Coast Guard polices harbors and enforces laws against smuggling.
   d. It maintains lighthouses and other technical aids to navigation.
   e. It stations weather ships at sea to supply information to aircraft as well as to ships at sea.
   f. In time of war, the Coast Guard becomes part of the United States Navy.
   g. As an international service the Coast Guard conducts the ice patrol in the North Atlantic and the Bering Sea.
   h. It establishes safety standards for yachts, motorboats, and other vessels.
   i. In World War II the Coast Guard furnished crews for many landing craft.

2. **The mineral wealth of Chile is outstanding.**

   a. The largest copper deposit in the world is at Chuquicamata, Chile.

   b.   The largest producer of copper is the United States.
   c.   There are other large copper deposits in central Chile.
   d.   Chile also has the world's largest deposits of natural nitrates.
   e.   Copper and nitrates are important Chilean exports, some 70 percent of its foreign trade.
   f.   Some insect sprays contain compounds of copper.
   g.   Chile leads South America in the mining of iron ore.
   h.   Other mineral deposits include oil, coal, sulfur, gold, tungsten, and manganese.

549   Coherence in the paragraph   results from the correct arrangement of the parts of a paragraph—an arrangement in which each part of the paragraph is often aided by the use of appropriate transitional words, but too many such words results in a heavy, stilted style. Careful arrangement is the important means of attaining coherence. Transition words are so numerous that one may be found to suit the exact need of almost any transition.

♦ **Transition words** are used to show: (a) passing of time; (b) addition; (c) contrast or opposition; (d) comparison and similarity; (e) concession, admission of facts; (f) sequence of numerical order; (g) result; (h) summary.

   Some of the more commonly used of these words and phrases are *furthermore, however, for this reason, consequently, in addition, notwithstanding, all things considered, to this end, hence, above all, for example, as a consequence, on the contrary, nevertheless, as a result, but, otherwise, yet, still, meanwhile, presently, finally, in conclusion, for instance, therefore,* and *accordingly.*

   The paragraph below illustrates the smooth use of transition words. In order to see the importance of arrangement, try placing the next to the last sentence as the concluding sentence. This will show the loss in force of the paragraph that is not coherent:

> You may be sure that I am pleased with the adjustment you have made about the returned goods. This adjustment is in keeping with the fine spirit of honesty and fairness that you have continually shown me in the years in which I have been doing business with you. As a consequence of your excellent treatment, I have continued to give you the bulk of my orders. In addition, I have used my influence to turn other business to you. As in the past, I shall continue to show you my appreciation in this practical way.

Exercise 5.2   Paragraph Coherence.
All of the sentences under each title below belong in a single paragraph. First find the sentence that best introduces the topic, and then seek the one that most logically follows. Follow this procedure until you have used all of the

sentences to form a coherent paragraph. List the rearranged sentence letters in their new sequences for each of the following three paragraphs:

Walk Down Any Street

a. The curtain rises on the old plots: boy meets girl, cops and robbers—familiar stories, but always with a new twist in the gritty theater of the street.
b. He hesitates between the raw night and the warmth of the subway.
c. A street is a theater where admission is free and the curtain is always going up.
d. Now he is gone into the darkness, and we can never know his story.
e. What plot is that old man acting out?
f. In this theater all the dramas are acted out clearly, yet remain mysteries.

Defender of the Law

a. But the observer would have been wrong.
b. A closer look at the burning eyes behind the mask, the reckless smile, the swaggering gait, would have revealed, not just plain Scotty Forbes, but the Lone Ranger.
c. When he stalked out again, a calloused adult observer might have thought him indistinguishable from thousands of other children.
d. The observer might have put him down as just another six-year-old in a black mask.
e. Scotty Forbes stalked into Jenkins' Toy Store with a grimy quarter clenched possessively in his fist.
f. He was the fearless defender of law and order all the way from Bedford Avenue to Barney's Supermarket.

Sterling

a. At that time the coins of England had decreased in value and contained little silver.
b. These coins were called Easterlings to distinguish them from the low-silver alloy coins of England.
c. The word *sterling* has been used to mean high-quality silver since the 1200's.
d. The only coins that contained large proportions of silver were those coined by the merchants of the Hanseatic League in northern Germany.
e. English speech quickly turned *Easterling* to *sterling*.

550   **Emphasis in the paragraph** results from giving stress to the important ideas. If more space is given to the important ideas than to the unimportant, there is possibility of interfering with unity and coherence; therefore it may be best to give emphasis by position. The beginning or the close of the paragraph is the most emphatic position. The paragraph below from "The Masque of the

Red Death," a short story by Poe, is a good illustration of proper emphasis in the paragraph. Note how by position the emphasis is given by *Red Death*. It is obvious that a shifting of the last sentence to the middle of the paragraph would weaken the entire effect:

> And now was acknowledged the presence of the Red Death. He had come like a thief in the night. And one by one dropped the revelers in the blood-bedewed halls of their revel, and each died in the despairing posture of his fall. And the life of the ebony clock went out with that of the last of the gay. And the flames of the tripods expired. And Darkness and Decay and the Red Death held illimitable dominion over all.

Exercise 5.3   Constructing Paragraphs.

Write paragraphs for two of the following topics, developing your ideas through strong descriptive details, concrete examples, or contrasting supporting evidence. Underline your topic sentences.

Topics	Possible Topic Sentences
a. **T-shirts**	T-shirts are our generation's most popular art form.
b. **The energy crisis**	Too many people view the energy crisis as only a temporary inconvenience.
c. **Intramural sports**	Intramural sports ought to be given more support than intercollegiate sports.
d. **Bumper stickers**	Today's bumper stickers are among the best indicators of public opinion.
e. **Politics**	My introduction to political reality came when. . . .
f. **Editorial cartoons**	The most important ingredients in editorial cartoons are. . . .
g. **Military service**	The voluntary armed forces offer. . . .

WRITING ESSAYS

551   ESSAYS   The term *essay* is a broad one, use here to include relatively themes or compositions (ranging in length from several paragraphs to several pages). They may be assigned as in-class themes or essay examinations, or they may be short creative writing inspired by personal reactions. Accordingly, their styles and tones will vary.

552   THE ESSAY AS A UNIT   It is necessary that not only the sentences and paragraphs each maintain unity, coherence, and emphasis but also that the composition as a whole maintain these three qualities. The essay must be a unit with its parts so arranged as to show clearly their relationship. In addition, the most important ideas must be in those positions that give them the greatest emphasis—the beginning and the close.

553   TOPIC TO THESIS   To obtain unity in your essay, you need to give direction to your topic, converting it from a topic to a *thesis*. A thesis for an essay is comparable to the topic sentence for a paragraph. (For a more detailed discussion of how to shape a thesis, see paragraph 591 in Chapter 7.)

EXAMPLE:	Topic	Thesis
	Market Gardening	Market gardening is a far more complicated process than most city dwellers realize.
	Tennis	Tennis is a particularly good game for students.

554   ORGANIZING MATERIAL   Writing an essay brings together all of the skills covered thus far in this text. Obviously you need to adhere to good grammatical and mechanical practices in writing an essay. As you combine well-written sentences into logically developed paragraphs, however, you need to be particularly conscious of how you organize this material toward a goal.

555   OUTLINING   An excellent starting point for your essay is to outline your planned development. Begin by jotting down all your thoughts and known facts on the subject as they occur to you—at first with no attempt at orderly arrangement, then with ideas gathered into related groups. An intermediate step, showing topics arranged in logical order, is furnished here for the subject of *market gardening*:

   a. Deciding what to plant
   b. Selecting the seed
   c. Preparing the soil
   d. Planting the seed
   e. Cultivating the growing plants
   f. Gathering the produce
   g. Preparing the produce for market
   h. Selling the produce

556   TOPIC OUTLINE   A topic outline is made up of headings which indicate the main ideas for the composition. Terms of the same rank should be parallel. Examples and supportive points should be subordinated. The most common form of outline uses Roman numerals for main topics, capital letters for subtopics, Arabic numerals for subdivisions of subtopics, and lower-case letters for a fourth subdivision if needed.

◆ Each set of topics and subtopics must be marked with the same type of symbol and worded in the same way. Never write a single subtopic—no *A* without a *B* and no *1* without a *2*—because a single subtopic is merely part of the topic. Subtopics are indented, and subdivisions of subtopics are double indented.

EXAMPLE: Subject: Olympic Games
Thesis: The Olympic Games have developed into one of the world's most spectacular international events.
Topic Outline: I. Ancient games, 776 B.C.–396 A.D.

    A. Origin in Greece
    B. Purpose
    C. Importance

  II. Modern revival, 1896

    A. Purpose
      1. Promotion of interest in education and culture
      2. Fostering of international understanding
    B. First modern Olympics
      1. Time and place
      2. Countries competing
    C. Later games
    D. Most recent games
      1. Time and place
      2. Countries competing
      3. Records established

Exercise 5.4 The Topic Outline.

Subject: Accidents. Thesis: The causes of accidents are many and varied. Place the following topics and subtopics in outline form. (The exact order will vary from student to student, but there will likely be a clear consensus in your class as to the groupings.) Use all of the following:

Poor eyesight of drivers, Poor headlights, Highway deficiencies, Playing in street, Reckless driving, Driver defects, Failure to use seatbelts, Unstandardized signs, Speed, Jaywalking, Defective brakes, Pedestrians' mistakes, Sharp turns, Failure to signal in traffic, Mechanical defects, Narrow roads, Darting from behind parked cars, Defective tires.

557 SENTENCE OUTLINES The sentence outline (less common) has complete sentences:

TENNIS IS A GOOD GAME FOR STUDENTS

  I. It provides pleasure.
    A. The change from study to play relieves tension.
    B. The thrill of competition is stimulating.
  II. It promotes health.
    A. The outdoor exercise is good for the body.
    B. The keen interest in the game keeps the brain alert.

III. It develops good citizenship.
    A. The contact with others discourages selfishness.
    B. The rules of the game make necessary a regard for the rights of others.

558 USING THE OUTLINE Remember that an outline's primary purpose is not to look pretty (with neat indentations and numerous subtopics) but rather to help you achieve unity and coherence in your writing. In most cases it is an organizing device, not an end in itself. Use it to see how best to order your ideas and facts; use it also to see at a glance whether you are including any material that, however true it might be, may not be relevant to your specific thesis.

Exercise 5.5   The Outline.
  A. The following topic outline represents a good start, but it lacks coherence and unity. Some topics are repeated or appear under the wrong headings. Some may be irrelevant. Copy this outline on a separate sheet, improving it by striking out the topics that should be omitted.

How to Write a Composition

  I. Selecting a subject
    A. Evaluating general interest
    B. Narrowing the topic
    C. Planning what to say
  II. Gathering material
    A. Finding sources
      1. Looking in the library
    B. Taking notes
      1. Arranging notes
      2. Filing notes
  III. Arranging material
    A. Arranging notes
    B. Making an outline
    C. Planning time to write
  IV. Developing the first draft
    A. Eliminating unimportant and irrelevant material
    B. Emphasizing most important ideas
    C. Deciding what to leave out
  V. Writing the final draft
    A. Rephrasing awkward sentences
    B. Deciding what to emphasize
    C. Making transitions smoother
    D. Proofreading for accuracy

  B. Construct a topic outline or a sentence outline for a subject of your own choosing. Be prepared to write an essay from your outline.

559   TITLES   Whenever possible, you should provide a title to distinguish your essay, even if the writing is fairly brief. A well-selected title serves at least two important functions: it can attract attention to the writing, and it can provide the reader a good indication of your thesis. The best titles are usually short and accurate. Since your title is the first chance you have to make an impression on your reader, you should devote some of your creative energy into making that impression as favorable as possible.

EXAMPLE: Possible titles for an essay on bumper stickers:

"Bumper Stickers"   (Accurate but dull)

"The Greatest Thing Since Sliced Bread"   (Clever, but vague; not indicative of thesis)

"If You're Close Enough to Read This. . ."   (Clever, but perhaps the allusion is too restricted to be widely enough known)

"Let Your Bumper Do the Talking"   (Good possibility)

Exercise 5.6   Titles.
Offer at least two possible titles for each of the following theses:

a. Every student ought to study art [or music, business, etc.] for at least one year.
b. Primitive peoples' fears about photography may have been justified.
c. Too many Americans today cannot afford proper medical care.
d. Job interviews require more preparation than most students realize.

560   ESSAY EXAMINATIONS   The basic rules of writing already discussed apply also, of course, to answering an essay examination. Since access to books during such examinations is often prohibited, however, study preparation is essential; and since time limitations are often in effect, organization becomes especially important. Some of the other considerations you should keep in mind include:

a. **Prepare Properly**. An essay needs to be supported with concrete facts, descriptions, etc. If a process has five steps, memorize them; you will need them in an essay just as much as you would in an objective examination.

b. **Follow Instructions**. Read the assignment carefully to locate the key word or words. There is a big difference, for instance, between *defining* something, *evaluating* it, or *comparing* it with something else. Don't waste your time spilling forth material that is irrelevant to what you have been asked to present.

c. **Think BEFORE Writing**. Before plunging into writing the essay, take a few minutes to jot down on scrap paper the basic points you want to make. Determine their most effective sequence, and then decide what your thesis will be (checking it against the instructions again to ensure its appropriateness). Usually you will not have time to prepare a formal outline, but the few minutes you devote here to organizing your material can be vital to the success of your essay examination.

FORMS OF DISCOURSE

561   There are four types of expression known as **forms of discourse**, and every paragraph illustrates one of these types or a combination of two or more of them. These four forms are **exposition, description, narration, argumentation.**

Exposition

562   **Exposition** is explaining, and it is the form most frequently used. It is, however, often closely associated with the other forms, particularly with description. In fact, exposition and description are so closely blended sometimes that it is difficult to distinguish between them. Exposition depends for its effectiveness on the use of accurate, concrete words instead of vague, abstract terms. The paragraph below illustrates clear exposition in very simple, accurate terms:

> When you speak, your vocal chords vibrate. The vibrations cause changes in the pressure of the air. Waves of sound are set up. When the sound waves reach another person, they strike the eardrum. The eardrum vibrates according to the changing pressure of the air on it. The person hears.

Description

563   **Description** is picturing in words. As has been pointed out (562), it is closely associated with the other forms, particularly exposition, with which it is often almost inseparably blended. Pure description is seldom met with in discourse, for it needs the other forms to give it movement. It is made vivid by the use of meaningful words, particularly adjectives (275) and nouns (39). The paragraph given below, from Irving's "Rural Life in England," is a good illustration of description. Note the descriptive words *imposing, vast, vivid, gigantic, rich, solemn, woodland, silent, natural, glassy, sequestered, quivering, yellow, sleeping, limpid, rustic, sylvan, green, dark, classic:*

> Nothing can be more imposing than the magnificence of English park scenery. Vast lawns that extend like sheets of vivid green, with here and there clumps of gigantic trees, heaping up rich piles of foliage: the solemn pomp of groves and woodland glades, with the deer trooping in silent herds across them; the hare bounding away to the covert; or the

pheasant, suddenly bursting upon the wing; the brook, taught to wind in natural meanderings or expand into a glassy lake; the sequestered pool, reflecting the quivering trees, with the yellow leaf sleeping on its bosom, and the trout roaming fearlessly about its limpid waters; while some rustic temple of sylvan statue, grown green and dank with age, gives an air of classic sanctity to the seclusion.

Narration

564 **Narration** is a rehearsal of events which may have been either real or imaginary; it is the telling of a story, whether the story is truth or fiction. This may be done best by the selection of events that are essential to the story, by the proper use of transitional expressions that show: (a) continuation of thought; (b) passing of time; (c) result; (d) opposition. It is usually associated with exposition and description, and it must give the effect of movement from event to event. The many stories with which we are familiar are examples of narration. Those who write or tell stories should observe these precautions for successful narration: **Make** a prompt, effective beginning; **stick** to the story; **tell** the story simply; **end** it promptly.

Point of view is another element that is of key importance in narration. First-person point of view (*I*) and third-person point of view (*he, she, they*) indicate either that the teller is an actor in the story or that the teller is an observer of a story about others. Consistency in the use of verb tenses and transitional words is essential, since they differ for the two points of view.

Argumentation

565 **Argumentation** is an effort to show by logical arrangement of facts that a statement is true or false, as in a mathematical demonstration such as the proof of a proposition in geometry. When one attempts to establish a new conviction in written matter, one explains facts favorable to that conviction: this is argumentation. To be successful in argumentation, one must exercise the same tact and skills as in the other forms. Much good may be achieved through written argumentation, but in the verbal contacts of everyday life, tact must be applied.

DEVELOPMENT OF CREATIVE EXPRESSION

566 **Creative expression** is the communication of a feeling or experience that is worth sharing with others just for its own sake. This is the type of expression which at its best gives us our literature. But all of us, whether or not we have the urge or the genius to become great creative artists, should give thought to creative expression, since it may help us to observe more closely the things about us. We become more critical of ourselves and others and thus better

able to analyze our own behavior and to be more sympathetic with the behavior of others. Through this type of expression we may eventually have a
broader understanding of life and its problems.

Précis-Writing

567   ABILITY TO CONDENSE EXPRESSION   It is important that one develop the
ability to express one's thoughts in well-organized paragraphs of the different
forms of discourse (561), and it is of no less importance that one should learn
how to condense one's meaning into the fewest possible words. The ability
to condense the expression of others to the fewest possible words should also
be acquired. Such a condensed form of expression retains the thought and
emphasis of the original and is called a **précis.**

568   THE PRÉCIS   A standard definition of the précis is a "brief summary of essential points, statements, or facts."   It differs from a **paraphrase** in that it is
much shorter and more precisely and accurately written. It must retain in
few words the ideas of the original, and these ideas must be clearly and forcefully expressed. The length of the précis may vary with the intensity of the
thought, but a good general average would be to reduce the number of words
to one third or one fourth the original. The writer of the précis must grasp
the entire meaning of the expression to be condensed.

569   SUGGESTIONS FOR PRÉCIS-WRITING   Précis-writing is excellent exercise for
inexperienced writers who have a tendency to wordiness (462). Here are
some general suggestions:

a.   Be sure you understand what you are trying to condense.
b.   Follow the original without changing the order of the thought.
c.   Use your own words.
d.   Write as clearly and forcefully as possible.

570   ILLUSTRATION   Below is an illustration of précis-writing in which each of five
summaries of a paragraph is rated by expert authority. The test paragraph,
given first, is followed by instructions for grading and five summaries. (The
extract is "Selection V, Form A" from the *Poley Précis Test,* a standard test
by Irwin C. Poley, Public School Publishing Company, Bloomington, Illinois.
Reprinted by permission of the publisher.)

> Vandalism in the parks is all too typical of one side of the American
> character. We seem incapable of bearing in mind an idea of decency in
> the abstract. As guests, if our host is a friend, we treat him with cour-
> tesy; but if he is unknown and not at hand to watch us we concede him
> no rights whatever; as hunters borrowing somebody's land we drop
> cigarettes and start forest fires; as campers borrowing somebody's
> woods we have a litter of cans and refuse that is notorious. . . . We are
> callous to the idea that things ought not to be destroyed, no matter
> who owns them or who will use them. . . . Park vandals are guests of

the public, and they should have enough regard for the host not to destroy his property. They use the parks in common with many other people and they should have a thought to the comfort of others.

Editorial, New York World.

INSTRUCTIONS: Below are five summaries of the paragraph just given. Try to rate the summaries as to accuracy and completeness. The ratings as given by the author of the test appear after the last summary.

a. Americans are apt to be discourteous in their treatment of public parks. They should remember that consideration is due as much to an absent or public host as to a present or private one.

b. In America the parks are littered with trash, especially cigarettes, which may start a forest fire. Private property should be respected as much as public.

c. Private property should be respected as much as public property, if not more. Parks are sure to be littered with refuse, and public camping sites are spoiled.

d. If hunters borrow land, they should be careful not to drop cigarettes and thus start a fire. Campers should not leave a litter of refuse behind them; even if they do not know the owner, they should be considerate of the property.

e. Americans should learn to get along pleasantly with people they meet in the park. The public is our host, and individuals should try to act as courteously to one another as they do in Europe.

The five summaries are rated as follows: *a* best expresses the thought of the original paragraph; *b, c,* and *e* are inaccurate (that is, they contain actual errors of statement); *d* is inadequate (that is, it misses the central thought of the original paragraph although it contains no error of statement).

Exercise 5.7 Summarizing or Précis Writing.
Read the article below and then write a précis of it in eighty words or less.

Carlsbad Caverns

Seven miles of underground trails lie ahead of you. Hidden electric lights provide a spooky illumination. As your party enters the caves, the guide supplies information about the size of the caves and their spectacular formations. He also tells of a cowboy named Jim White, who discovered the caverns in 1901.

The air grows chilly and damp. At 180 feet below the surface, you pass by a murky cavern where furry bodies can be dimly seen—millions of bats. You peer fearfully into black wells—unexplored holes of un-known depths. Rock formations seem to resemble fantastic animals. Going ever deeper, you see giant stalactites hanging from the ceiling like icicles. Equally large stalagmites sprout from the floor. Some stalac-tites and stalagmites are joined, forming immense pillars as of palaces.

The caves have names to fit: King's Palace, Queen's Chamber, Papoose's Chamber.

Seven or eight hundred feet below the surface, there is the "Big Room." More than a half mile long and nearly 300 feet high, it contains a stalagmite called Giant Dome, which is sixty million years old. In the Big Room you sit down cozily together—and suddenly the lights go out! This is absolute darkness.

In a moment the lights go on again. You are led to a dining room for food and rest. This is supposed to be the halfway mark. By now, you are chilly, tired, and limping, and you have seen enough for one day. You cut short your underground trip by taking a modern elevator to the entrance hall.

Critical Reading

571   READING   "There is an art of reading, as well as an art of thinking, and an art of writing." This aphorism by Isaac D'Israeli, written in 1791, is still as valid as when it was written. Critical reading has the major task of grasping the thought of the writer; a secondary task is observing the mechanical techniques used in expressing it. These techniques include the spelling, grammar, punctuation, and capitalization employed in writing down the thoughts. A reading of this kind is referred to as proofreading.

572   READING FOR THOUGHT   Reading for content may be done for a number of reasons. One may read the newspapers as a daily habit for the current events reported there. Or one may read magazines and books from a desire to learn about the opinions and experiences of others or to enlarge personal horizons.

A more serious purpose of the reader may be to gather material for a paper or a speech through extensive reading in a library. The latter type of reading is usually accompanied with note-taking, the purpose of which is to gather facts.

Every reader should learn to grasp and quickly pinpoint the main ideas while reading. The principal facts in a newspaper article may be learned by reading the headlines and lead paragraphs. One should train oneself to glean from every paragraph the necessary facts by writing brief, clear notes or a précis (567). Accurate reading and expert précis-writing go hand in hand, both being invaluable aids to anyone who wishes to attain effective expression.

573   PROOFREADING   In addition to learning to get the thought from written expression, one must learn to detect mechanical errors in it. Reading for the purpose of correcting mechanical errors is called **proofreading**, though in the strictest sense this term is applied only to the correction of proof sheets for a printer. You may use any simple system of marking errors in proofreading your own work or the work of others. Appropriate rules for correcting such errors are to be found in the various sections of this book.

Using the Library

A knowledge of how to use the rich resources of a library is one of the most essential parts of a good education. The following pages will present some of the basic principles that should help you in making those resources available to you. Be aware, however, that libraries vary greatly in size of collection, organization, physical arrangements, user regulations, etc.

To use your library most efficiently you need to allow time to become familiar with its particular physical setup and organizing principles. Check at the main desk or information counter to determine whether the library offers a handbook or guide to assist users. The time you take to familiarize yourself initially with the strengths and special requirements of your library will probably prove to be a valuable investment later when you need to research specific assignments.

THE CARD CATALOG

574 Regardless of the size of your library, the central information point will be its card catalog: the index to that library's holdings. Here you should be able to determine fairly quickly what major resources are available on any given author or subject. This information, on 3" X 5" index cards, is filed alphabetically by 1) author, 2) title, and 3) subject. For most books, then, there will be at least three separate cards within the catalog. (Note: In some libraries all cards are filed in a single alphabetical file; in others you may find that the subject catalog is separate from the author and title cards.)

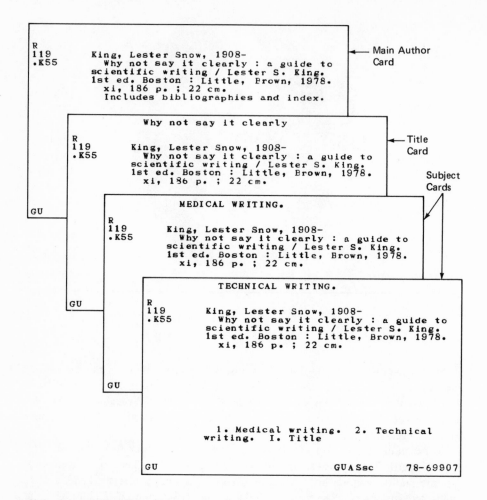

575 CALL NUMBERS In the upper left-hand corner of each card-catalog card is the identification number for the book it represents. This call number appears also on the spine or binding of the book itself and serves to designate where the book is shelved within the library. Obviously it is important that you accurately record this call number—line by line—if you hope to find that particular book among the many thousands within the library.

576 The call numbers are usually based upon one of the two primary classification systems: the Dewey Decimal System or the Library of Congress classification system. Some knowledge of both systems is valuable, since both are in widespread use. Many libraries, in fact, are now using the Library of Congress system for new books, while retaining the Dewey system for those books already cataloged.

577 The Dewey Decimal System classifies all works exclusive of fiction into ten major groups and divides each group further into ten subgroups. The major groups are as follows:

000-099   General works, such as encyclopedias
100-199   Philosophy, psychology
200-299   Religion, mythology
300-399   Social sciences, such as government, sociology, economics, and books on clubs, holidays, and etiquette
400-499   Languages: grammar, linguistics
500-599   Pure science: mathematics, physics, chemistry, botany, zoology, earth science, biological sciences
600-699   Applied science: inventions, gardening, cooking, sewing, aeronautics, engineering, medicine, agriculture
700-799   Arts and recreation: such as drawing, painting, and music
800-899   Literature (except fiction)
900-999   History: travel, geography, biography

578   **The Library of Congress classification system** is more precise in its ability to classify books and is found more frequently in larger libraries. It uses letters of the alphabet to indicate general topic headings, followed by additional letters and Arabic numerals to classify more specifically. Only the major classes are listed here:

A   General Works
B   Philosophy, Psychology, Religion
C   Auxiliary Sciences of History
D   History: General and Old World
E and F   History: America
G   Geography, Anthropology, Recreation
H   Social Sciences
J   Political Science
K   Law
L   Education
M   Music and Books on Music
N   Fine Arts
P   Language and Literature
Q   Science
R   Medicine
S   Agriculture
T   Technology
U   Military Science
V   Naval Science
Z   Bibliography, Library Science

GENERAL REFERENCE COLLECTION

579   A good starting point for all research—and often an essential one—is the general reference collection available in your library. Here—usually in one location—are gathered the works that attempt to collect and classify specific pieces of information. These include dictionaries, atlases, encyclopedias, bibliographies, biographical collections, and other specialized groupings of data that may be exactly what you need to initiate your research.

It's worth taking the time to learn what reference works are in print by checking the most recent edition of Constance M. Winchell's *Guide to Reference Books.* Available in virtually all college libraries, it provides a listing with brief descriptions of most general and specific reference works. Remember always to check the copyright date of the work cited and try to find the latest edition. Even good reference books can lose their value as they become dated, so you should try to consult the most current sources. Some of the most frequently consulted reference works are listed by category in the following paragraphs. Consult your library holdings to obtain full bibliographic information for the most recent editions available there.

580　GENERAL UNABRIDGED DICTIONARIES

A Dictionary of American English on Historic Principles.
Funk and Wagnalls New Standard Dictionary.
New Century Dictionary.
The Oxford English Dictionary (commonly referred to as the *O.E.D.*: sometimes called the *N.E.D.*, since it was originally entitled *A New English Dictionary on Historical Principles* when it was first published, 1883–1933).
The Random House Dictionary of the English Language.
Webster's Third New International Dictionary.

581　GENERAL ENCYCLOPEDIAS Encyclopedias usually issue supplemental texts (often annually) to keep their primary editions up to date. Once again, you need to check the date of the edition you are using, and then consult any subsequent supplements for more recent information.

Collier's Encyclopedia.
Encyclopedia Americana.
Encyclopedia Britannica.
World Book Encyclopedia.

582　SPECIAL ENCYCLOPEDIAS Whatever your special area of interest, there is a good chance you can locate a special encyclopedia dealing with it directly or closely related to it. Check the listings under encyclopedias in Winchell's *Guide to Reference Books* or the latest volume of the *Cumulative Book Index.* Most special encyclopedias are not updated as regularly as general encyclopedias, and some of them may be quite dated. Note: not all of these works contain the word *encyclopedia* in their titles (e.g., *Grove's Dictionary of Music and Musicians*), but they function effectively as encyclopedic collections of information. The following samples are intended to indicate the wide range of subjects covered in available special encyclopedias.

The Catholic Encyclopedia.
Encyclopedia of Education.
Encyclopedia of Sociology.
Encyclopedia of World Art.
Encyclopedia of World Literature in the Twentieth Century.
International Encyclopedia of Social Sciences.
The Jewish Encyclopedia.
McGraw-Hill Encyclopedia of Science and Technology.
Oxford Classical Dictionary.
Van Nostrand's Scientific Encyclopedia.

583   ATLASES AND GAZETTEERS   With national boundaries continuing to change and new nations emerging each year, it is important that you consult the most recent editions of atlases available. Most of those cited here are updated frequently.

Encyclopedia Britannica World Atlas.
National Atlas of the United States (U.S. Geological Survey).
National Geographic Atlas of the World.
The New York Times Atlas of the World.
Rand-McNally New Cosmopolitan World Atlas.

584   YEARBOOKS AND ALMANACS

Americana Annual (1923 to date)
Britannica Book of the Year (1938 to date).
Guinness Book of World Records (1955 to date).
Information Please Almanac (1947 to date).
The Official Associated Press Almanac (1970 to date).
Statesman's Year-Book (1864 to date).
World Almanac and Book of Facts (1868 to date).

585   BIOGRAPHICAL INFORMATION

Biography Index (1947 to date).
Contemporary Authors (1962 to date).
Current Biography: Who's News and Why (1940 to date).
Dictionary of American Biography (1928-43 with supplements).
Dictionary of National Biography [British] (1938 with supplements).
International Who's Who (1935 to date).
Who's Who (1848 to date).
Who's Who in America (1899 to date).

INDEXES TO PERIODICALS AND NEWSPAPERS

586   Just as the card catalog is the key to a library's collection of books, so the periodical indexes (usually located in the reference room) serve to locate articles that appeared in magazines and journals. Check the introductory pages

of each of the indexes you consult to learn the format and abbreviations employed. Most useful of the indexes are the following:

Book Review Digest.

Humanities Index (1974 to date), a continuation of the *Social Sciences and Humanities Index* (1965-73), previously titled the *International Index* (1907-65).

The New York Times Index (1913 to date)—a particularly useful tool to determine the date of a specific event, which can then be researched not only in the *Times* but also in other papers and journals that were published at or about the same time.

Reader's Guide to Periodical Literature (1900 to date).

Social Sciences Index (1974 to date), a continuation of the *Social Sciences and Humanities Index* (1965-73) and the *International Index* (1907-65).

Note: While these indexes occasionally overlap in references, they basically index from different sources. *The Reader's Guide,* for instance, serves as an index to over 100 popular magazines, while the *Humanities Index* draws many of its entries from more learned journals.

587   There are, in addition, a number of **special periodical indexes** (covering more narrowly defined areas) and indexes which provide brief abstracts of articles (e.g., in Biology, Chemistry, English Studies, Psychology, etc.). Some of the more established of these include the following:

Art Index (1929 to date).

Biography Index (1946 to date).

Biological and Agricultural Index (1964 to date, a continuation of the *Agricultural Index* (1916-64).

Education Index (1929 to date).

Engineering Index (1884 to date).

Music Index (1949 to date).

Public Affairs Information Service (1915 to date)—political science sociology, economics.

588   Once you have located in an index the title of a periodical article you wish to consult, be sure to record the full bibliographical data given. For now you need to determine whether your library receives that periodical and—if they do—where you can locate it. Most libraries have special periodical rooms for the current issues of magazines and journals. Older issues, however, are bound in hardcover and are usually shelved within the general book collection. Since the card catalog for a library's periodical holdings is often separate from the main catalog, you may need to consult with the reference librarian to complete your search successfully.

The Research Paper

The research paper is the most extensive kind of writing many people will ever perform. Often called a "term paper" in college (or an "investigative report" in business), the research paper is far more than a jumbled collection of facts and quotations dealing with one subject. A good research paper (usually 1,000 to 5,000 words in length) deals thoroughly with its announced topic, demonstrates a clear sense of purpose, and identifies the sources of the information used in its writing.

589 The major steps in preparing a research paper are as follows: 1) selecting a subject; 2) narrowing focus and defining purpose; 3) studying available source material; 4) planning an outline; 5) writing the paper; and 6) revising the paper and preparing final copy. It is worth noting that over half of these steps involve vital "pre-writing" preparation.

590 SELECTING THE SUBJECT The most important element in topic selection is its interest to you and to your readers. It is usually wise to choose something with which you already have some familiarity, a topic in which your interest is real. This will make the process of writing more enjoyable for you and is likely also to make your final product more inviting for your readers. At this point it is valuable to make a preliminary survey of materials available in your library. This will help to ensure that sufficient resources are at hand; it will also assist in the next stage, limiting the scope of your investigation.

591   NARROWING THE FOCUS AND DEFINING PURPOSE   General topics like ecology, sports, aviation, education, or literature may well attract your interest, but they are obviously too broad in scope to be dealt with in an ordinary research paper. They need to be reduced in focus to manageable proportions. Even when a general topic is assigned to you by your instructor or employer, you often need to narrow the scope of your research.

♦ **EXAMPLE:**   General topic—Medical Care

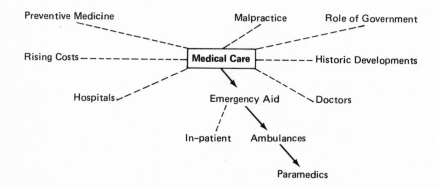

Once your focus is narrowed, in this case to paramedics, you need to give it a directional purpose. What do you honestly want to say about your subject? What is your purpose in writing?

♦ **Weak:**   I want to discuss recent local interest in paramedics.
I plan to examine the pros and cons of paramedics.

♦ **Stronger:**   Paramedics are . . . a waste of taxpayer's money.
. . . the trend of the future.
. . . a vital part of our medical care system.
. . . badly undertrained.

Note that in the first examples given here the announced *subject* is actually used in the sentence as an *object of a preposition;* the purpose of the paper seems vague. However, when the paper's subject also serves as the subject of the sentence (forming a *thesis*), the writer's intent becomes clearer, and the research paper now has a sense of purpose and direction. Both the writer and the reader understand that the rest of the paper is going to provide evidence to support that statement.

592   STUDYING AVAILABLE SOURCE MATERIALS   At this point you need to make extensive use of your library's resources. Since you have already narrowed your topic and given it tentative directional focus, your efforts can now be devoted to finding that material that is most relevant to your specific goal. Try to be as systematic as possible in recording your research, so that you won't need to repeat your work later.

593   **The Source Card Technique**   List each source on a separate card—usually 3 X 5 inches. Include—

   a.   **Author's name.**   Give last name first, then given names, or the editor's name followed by the abbreviation *Ed.* When no author is given, list the title first.

   b.   **Title.**   Underline the title of a book, magazine, or newspaper and put quotation marks around the title of an article or chapter.

   c.   **Publication data.**   For book titles include the city where published, name of publisher, and copyright date. For magazines or journals use the volume number, date of issue, and page numbers.

   d.   **Library call number.**   For books include the call number so that you don't have to look this up again. Here are samples of source cards for a book, an article in a magazine, and an article in an encyclopedia:

> 610
> W
> Williams, Roger J.
> Threat against Disease,
> Environmental Prevention,
> New York: Pitman Publishing
> Corporation, 1971

> Young, Gordon, "Pollution,
> Threat to Man's Only Home,"
> National Geographic, Vol. 138,
> No. 6, December 1970, pp. 738-780

> Gates, David M., "Ecology,"
> Encyclopedia Americana (1976),
> Vol. 9, pp. 588-593.

594   **Taking Notes**   The best way to gather material is to take notes on 4" X 6" cards for which you have a file box. These cards will enable you to organize your material and refer readily to your information on each topic as you write. The following are helpful rules for taking notes:

   a.   **Use a separate card for each note.**   This permits you to file your cards under the proper topic. Sometimes more than one card will be necessary for a topic.

b. **Take thorough notes on all of the points you plan to cover.** Many students find that three or four good notes are required for every page of the research paper. Don't keep repeating information even if it is found in different books, and do not take notes on material you do not plan to use.

c. **List the topic the note refers to.** The topic is best placed at the top left corner of the card. This enables you to refer to your notes quickly as you write and helps you to organize your material.

d. **Be accurate.** Your notes must report facts, figures, opinions, and quotations accurately. Double-check every word and every figure with your source. Give enough detail so that you yourself can understand what you have written.

e. **Mark each direct quotation clearly.** Put quotation marks around each short quotation. Longer quotations are shown by leaving larger margins (510). Take down the exact words, punctuation, and capitalization. Use three dots to indicate the omission of parts of a quotation (488). Use direct quotations only if you plan to give the exact opinion of an authority or if the same idea cannot possibly be expressed in your own words. Too many quotations will make a very weak paper. Express your own ideas in your own way.

f. **Identify the source and give the page reference for each note.** This information will be necessary for your footnotes (599) and your bibliography (601). You should have some key for connecting your note card with its source card. You may make up your own abbreviation for each source card, or you may number your source cards in order and then put the proper source number on each note card.

595 **PLANNING AN OUTLINE** From your earliest consideration of a subject you ought to be jotting down—"brainstorming"—ideas for organizing your paper. These should evolve into a rough working outline, ordering the various elements you plan to cover. As you gather more material, you will probably make changes in the ordering sequence, omitting some of the aspects about which you can find little source material and adding others that appear to be more pertinent or interesting. After you complete your major study of available source material, you should be able to make your final outline (555-558) to guide your writing. It is helpful as you do this to remember your chosen thesis (the purpose of your writing) by making sure that the final outline is consistent with your overall goal.

596 **WRITING THE PAPER** If you have proceeded carefully through the various steps listed to this point, you ought to be ready to write. Now your "prewriting" work will prove invaluable, as you follow your outline in presenting the results of your research. Write in your own words as much as possible; avoid merely stringing together a number of quotations from outside sources.

Your first draft may be written fairly rapidly. Then you will probably find it necessary to amplify some portions and supply transitions (549)—sometimes using whole paragraphs—to make your paper a unified, coherent whole. By this point you should recognize that good writing is not a one-step affair: most first drafts are reworked extensively before they reach their final form.

597 REVISING AND PREPARING THE FINAL COPY The final drafts of a research paper provide an excellent opportunity to make useful stylistic modifications. Try to make your sentences work together to avoid their appearing as a miscellaneous assortment hastily compiled. Work to achieve a concise, yet inviting style by varying the sentence length and structure (421–431). Review the draft closely to correct any errors in the mechanics of composition or spelling. (Use your dictionary to check every word you use, if necessary.)

Unless instructed otherwise, you should prepare the final version of your research paper in typed form. Leave adequate margins (at least a one-inch space on each side, top, and bottom), and double-space lines (except for extended quotations of ten lines or more, which should be indented and single-spaced). Most research papers now present all documentation (footnotes and bibliography) on separate pages at the end of the paper, but check with your instructor on this and other questions of format. Regardless of the format employed, however, you are responsible for making your copy as attractively clean and legible as possible. Proofread carefully to ensure that all typographical errors are corrected, that all pages are numbered correctly, and that the total product is one in which you can take pride.

598 DOCUMENTATION: FOOTNOTES AND BIBLIOGRAPHY Since much of the material used in your research paper is likely to have come from the published work of others, it is important that you give complete and proper credit to these sources. Such acknowledgment serves as a directional aid to readers who want further information; it also protects you from the charge of plagiarism (literary theft). Obviously you need not credit general information that can easily be found in a number of different books. You should, however, document your major sources, not only for all direct quotations, but also for key ideas that you have borrowed and rephrased into your own words. The number of footnotes needed and the length of your bibliography will vary widely from one paper to another, depending upon the complexity of the subjects being treated.

599 Footnotes Footnotes are usually numbered consecutively throughout a research paper. At the end of a quotation (or other material to be credited), place a number slightly above the line to correspond with the number you will use as a footnote reference. Although footnotes were formerly placed at the bottom of their appropriate pages, the more common practice now (not only in research papers, but in many scholarly books as well) is to collect them at the end of the work. More important than location, however, are the accuracy and clarity of the documentation, as well as the consistency of the footnote format used throughout the paper. The following are examples of the most frequently encountered types of footnotes, using (with minor modifications) the format recommended in *The MLA Style Sheet*, 2nd ed. (New York: Modern Language Association of America, 1970):

♦ Books by a single author:

[1] Jack Matthews, *Collecting Rare Books for Pleasure and Profit* (New York: G.P. Putnam's Sons, 1977), pp. 200-201.

[Note: If the author's full name appears in your text, it may be omitted in the note. Similarly, if both the author's name and the title are used in the text immediately prior to the footnote reference, both may be omitted in the note itself.]

♦ Books by multiple authors and/or books prepared by editors:

[2] Sir Robert Howard and George Villiers, Second Duke of Buckingham, *The Country Gentleman: A "Lost" Play and Its Background,* ed. Arthur H. Scouten and Robert D. Hume (Philadelphia: Univ. of Pennsylvania Press, 1976), p. 33.

♦ Books of two or more volumes:

[3] Winston S. Churchill, *A History of the English Speaking Peoples* (New York: Dodd, Mead & Co., 1958), 4, 392.

[Note: The citation here is to Volume IV of the set. Conventional practice now calls for Roman numerals to be converted to Arabic (i.e., IV to 4) in documenting research. Note also that the page number(s) follow the volume number without the usual abbreviation indicator.]

♦ Separate titled elements within a book:

[4] Paul Zimmer, "Zimmer Envying Elephants," *The Zimmer Poems* (Washington, D.C.: Dryad Press, 1976), p. 41.

♦ Essays (or stories, poems, articles, etc.) in journals:

[5] Walker Percy, "Random Thoughts on Southern Literature, Southern Politics, and the American Future," *The Georgia Review,* 32 (1978), 499-511.

[Note: The date for Volume XXXII is provided as an additional aid to the reader.]

♦ **Articles in weekly magazines:**
    [6]Harry Waters and others, "Keeping Fit: America Tries to Shape Up," *Newsweek,* 23 May 1977, p. 78.

[Note: If there are a large number of authors, it is not necessary to list them all in the footnote, although you will ordinarily do so in the bibliography. If this were an unsigned article, the form would remain the same, except that it would begin with the title of the article.]

♦ **Articles in newspapers:**
    [7]George McGovern, "Probe Big Oil–Now," *The New York Times,* 1 Aug. 1979, p. A23, cols. 1-2.

♦ **Articles in encyclopedias:**
    [8]David M. Gates, "Ecology," *Encyclopedia Americana* (1976), 9, 588-93.

600 Subsequent References to Sources Footnoted When you refer several times to the same source, it is neither necessary nor desirable to repeat the entire footnote.   Every effort should be made to keep the footnotes from overwhelming your text.   Whenever possible, incorporate subsequent references within the text itself, inserting the page numbers within parentheses.   Otherwise, simply provide a short note indicating the author's last name and the page reference (adding an abbreviated title only if you cite more than one work by that author):

    [9]Percy, p. 503.   [10]Waters, p. 81.

In older books and journals you are likely to find footnotes using Latin terms, such as *Ibid.* ("in the same place"), *Loc. cit.* ("in the place cited"), *Op. cit.* ("in the work cited"), etc. Use of such terms is now far less common and should be avoided.   Keep your documentation clear, concise, and unpretentious.

601 Bibliography At the end of your research paper you should provide a list of all source material used in preparing your paper. Identify it clearly as, for example, "A List of Works Consulted," or "A Brief Bibliography," or "A Selected Bibliography."   It should include, at a minimum, all of the works cited in footnotes, but you should list as well any additional useful sources that you consulted but did not have to credit specifically.   Arrange your source cards in alphabetical order and then copy the information accurately.
    Note that there are some small but important differences between the footnote format and that used in standard bibliographic entries:

Name in   *Commas between*   *Main*   *Colon*   *Subtitle (often*
normal order   *main entries*   *title*   *before subtitle*   *omitted in footnotes)*

Footnote: [1] Lionel Trilling,   The Liberal Imagination: Essays on Literature and

No comma   *Place of*   *Publisher*   *Date of*   *Specific reference*
before   *publication*   *publication*   *(Always end note*
parenthesis   *Colon*   *with period)*

Society   (New York   :   Viking Press,   1950),   p.144.

Last name   *Period*   *Same as footnote format, except that subtitle*
first for   *must be furnished in full*
alphabetizing

Bibliography: Trilling, Lionel.   The Liberal Imagination: Essays on Literature

Period   *Same order as in footnote,*   *Always close*
        but without parentheses   *with a period*

and Society.   New York: Viking Press, 1950.

The Letter

Comparatively few people become full-time professional writers, but nearly all of us have occasion to write letters, and frequently these letters are of great personal or business importance. Obviously you should try to write your letters so that they project your writing at its best in appearance, correctness, and overall effectiveness. Beyond this, however, you need to be cognizant of the conventions and formats used in special kinds of letter writing.

602 SOCIAL LETTERS The different types of correspondence regarded as social letters range from highly formal invitations, acceptances, and regrets to very informal personal notes to close friends. The only special formats used here are in the formal social letters, for which you should consult one of the current guides to etiquette. Other social letters have no prescribed forms, although you should apply common-sense restrictions of your own to ensure that all your writing is legible and clearly understandable.

BUSINESS CORRESPONDENCE

603 The business letter has a clear purpose: to convey information. It should be as brief as is consistent with clarity and courtesy. Although its format is flexible enough to admit adjustments for special circumstances, it has become largely standardized in format, and the conventionally accepted practices should be followed when possible. This does not mean, however, that you should adopt hackneyed expressions that were once regularly associated with business correspondence. In particular, avoid such relics as

and oblige, as per, at hand, beg to state, early date, enclosed herewith, esteemed favor, has come to hand, kind favor, please note, recent date, we thank you kindly, we would advise, your favor of, yours to hand.

604 PARTS OF THE BUSINESS LETTER   There are six main parts of a business letter: **heading, inside address, salutation, body, complimentary close, signature.**   Other parts of the business letter which might be included are the initials placed at the left lower margin of a dictated letter to indicate the dictator and the stenographer, or typist, and the outside address (on the envelope). Each of these parts require separate discussion.

605 HEADING OF THE BUSINESS LETTER   If the stationery does not have a printed letterhead, the heading is placed at the upper right-hand corner and consists of the exact address of the writer and the date. Its length may vary, but it usually consists of three or four lines. The first line should give the smallest division, such as box number, name of building, or street and number; then comes the name of the city and the state, followed by the Zip Code number. The last line is reserved for the date.

The date may be stated correctly in either of two ways: 26 June 1965 or June 26, 1965. The first form is rapidly gaining acceptance as preferred, but many firms still retain the older format.

You may abbreviate the name of the state but not the city, and write the street number in figures. Today's writers do not abbreviate the name of the month in headings. Of course, where printed stationery is used, the letterhead includes all the heading except the date. The day of the month and the year are usually written in figures.

♦ The heading may be either of the block type or the indented. In the block type each line begins exactly the same distance from the right and left margins; in the indented type each succeeding line is spaced uniformly to the right. Examples are given below. The block form is almost always used in typing; the indented form may be used when writing in longhand:

1255 Walnut Street	1255 Walnut Street
Denver, Colorado 80202	Denver, Colorado 80202
15 December 19—	December 15, 19—

606 INSIDE ADDRESS   The inside address should be placed at the left margin below the heading; and it should give the proper courtesy title and business title, if any, correct name, and complete address of the person for whom the letter is intended. The form should be the same as that of the heading.

Mr. William Henderson
President
Mansfield Transport, Inc.
230 Mansfield Drive
New York, N.Y. 10020

Professor W. H. Wishmeyer
Department of English
Dickinson College
Carlisle, Pa. 17013

607   SALUTATION   The salutation is placed at the left margin two spaces below the inside address. The following are appropriate salutations in greeting an individual whose name is known: *Dear Mr._____, Dear Mrs._____, Dear Ms._____, Dear Miss_____.* In letters addressed to a firm or to an individual whose name is not known, *Dear Sir or Madam* is still the most common greeting.

♦ **Capitalization of the Salutation**   If the salutation consists of but two words, both are capitalized; but in a salutation such as *My dear General Smith*, the *dear* is not capitalized.

♦ **Punctuation of the Salutation**   The punctuation mark used after the salutation in a business letter is the colon (494). There is a present trend to add friendliness to the business letter; therefore the comma, less formal than the colon, might be used after the salutation of the more informal business letter to a friend.

608   BODY   The body of the letter is the message. It should conform to all rules of good writing. The sentences should be made effective, and the paragraphs should be short and forceful. All words should be well chosen, and each should add something to the effectiveness of the letter. Be careful to avoid the worn-out expressions that brand a letter as stilted. Make your letter a part of you—give it your personality.

The opening sentence is especially vital, for on its effectiveness may depend the fate of the entire message. The first sentence should be specific, and it should make some personal appeal to the reader. It should stress *you*, not *I*. It should never begin with any of the following meaningless references to the receipt of a letter: *Pursuant to your request of the fifth, Answering your letter of October 5, We beg to acknowledge receipt of your letter of June 4, We are in receipt of your letter of May 9, Your letter of recent date at hand, Acknowledging yours of recent date, Supplementing your letter of March 16, We have your letter of April 3, Replying to yours of August 12, Complying with your request of recent date, Referring to your favor of June 6.* Such expressions were once acceptable but they are now in the scrap heap of clichés except in certain legal correspondence.

The closing sentence is also very important. It should leave the reader feeling that he or she has just made contact with a cordial, friendly person.

When a letter is more than a page in length, the name of the person addressed, the page number, and the date should be placed at the top of each additional page. The margins should be the same for all pages. Five lines or more should appear on the last page.

609   COMPLIMENTARY CLOSE   The complimentary close should be consistent with the other parts of the letter. It should never be preceded by the participial expressions once so popular, such as *Thanking you for your favor, Hoping this will be satisfactory, Awaiting your reply.* The last sentence should be complete, and it should say something vital. The close needs no such outdated expressions as *I am* or *I remain* as an introduction. End the message with a forceful, appropriate sentence; then begin the close about the center of the page below. The following are correct in business letters: *Yours truly, Very truly yours, Yours sincerely, Sincerely yours, Sincerely.* The first word only of the close is capitalized. The close is punctuated with a comma at the end.

610   SIGNATURE   The signature is placed just below the close. Place the signature so that its first letter is below the first letter of the close. Usually the writer's name is also typed just beneath the longhand signature or with the initials of the typist at the left. Every letter should, of course, be signed in ink. The signature of a letter sent out by a business organization may include the name and position of the writer. The following are examples:

Sincerely,

Betty Lee Sargent

Betty Lee Sargent
Assistant Editor

♦ In signing a business letter, a married woman or a widow uses her own name, such as *Ann Clarke Brown*, not her married social name, *Mrs. Frank R. Brown.* She may write *Mrs.* in parentheses before the name or she may write her married name in parentheses below the signature:

Style 1
(Mrs.) Louise C. Randall

Style 2   *Louise C. Randall*
(Mrs. Robert J. Randall)

♦ In a dictated letter initials are typed at the lower left margin to identify the dictator and the stenographer. If there is an enclosure, it is indicated just under the initials; if more than one by ( ):

FBJ:RHM   FBJ/rhm   FBJ–RHM
Encl.   Encl.   Encl. (3)

611 APPEARANCE OF THE BUSINESS LETTER A business letter is usually typewritten on a sheet of good quality, white paper, 8½ x 11 inches. Double
spacing is used between parts of the letter and between paragraphs. The typing should be so placed on the sheet as to have the margins properly propor-
tioned, with the result that the typed text appears on the sheet much as
does a picture properly set in a frame. Even when a letter conforms to all the
other requirements of a good letter, its visual appearance also is important.
Either the block form (no indentations) or the semiblock style, in which the
paragraphs are indented (usually five spaces), is used by most business houses.
The following letter is in the semiblock style:

```
                                  126 Park Place
                                  Torrance, California 90507
                                  12 May 19__


        Mr. J. D. Foster
        1770 Pearl Street
        Denver, Colorado 80202


        Dear Mr. Foster:

             The information that you gave enabled me to
        obtain the Greeley contract that I had feared could
        not be concluded this spring. It was generous of
        you to take the trouble to assemble this data for me.

             As soon as I have checked the specifications, I
        will see you for the final details. You will agree
        with me, I know, that the outlook is promising for us.

             Unless I meet with some unexpected delay, I
        should have this preliminary work completed by the
        end of the week. I will let you know the day and the
        hour to expect me.


                                  Sincerely yours,

                                  L. W. Whitman

        LWW:pb                    L. W. Whitman
```

612 Folding the Letter The business letter is generally written on one side of a sheet of paper of commercial size, 8½ by 11 inches. When this is to be enclosed in an envelope of the larger size (usually No. 10—4 1/8 by 9 1/2 inches), fold up from the bottom about one third and down from the top slightly less. If the envelope to be used is of the smaller size (usually No. 6 3/4—3 5/8 by 6 1/2 inches), fold the lower part of the sheet over the upper so that the horizontal crease is slightly below the center; then fold the right-hand part so that the vertical crease is about one third from the right; then fold from the left so that the second vertical crease is slightly less than one third the width of the sheet from the left. Be sure that all folds are straight and that all edges are even. The good effect of a letter may be lessened by careless or slovenly folding.

613 Outside Address The outside address, or address on the envelope, should be the same in content as the inside address. The first line gives the name and the title of the person addressed, the second line gives the street number, and the third line gives the name of the city, the state, and the Zip Code number. The first line should be about the center of the envelope from top to bottom, though some writers prefer that it be slightly below. The name should be correctly spelled (a misspelled name is unforgivable!), and it should be written exactly as the one addressed is known to use it. If a business title is long, it should be placed on a separate line. Abbreviations are optional, but some careful writers avoid them, preferring to write out such words as the names of states, streets, and avenues. An address is usually single-spaced. Special directions, such as General Delivery and Personal, are placed in the lower left corner. The writer's name and address should be in the upper left corner. The following illustration is correct:

```
H. L. Wilson
2145 Valleyroad Avenue South
Springfield, Missouri 65804



              Mr. Frank W. Whitfield
              118 Spring Street Northwest
              Atlanta, Georgia 30304
```

Special Kinds of Business Letters

614 LETTER OF APPLICATION This letter should conform to all requirements of a good business letter, and in form it should be correct in every detail. No one should do less than one's very best in writing a letter of application. It is in reality a self-sale letter in which the writer is trying to sell services. A short letter of application may consist of three or four paragraphs. The first may mention the source of information about the position, the second may give facts that indicate one's qualifications for holding the position, the third may list references, and the fourth may suggest a possible conference or further communication. But even the conventional form of application may be altered to suit the originality of the writer and the type of position sought. The more individual the message, providing it is always sincere and sensible, the more evident the fitness to fill a position requiring originality.

```
                                    216A Franklin House
                                    University of Pennsylvania
                                    Philadelphia, PA 19104
                                    16 February 19__


      Ms. Joan Hamilton
      Personnel Manager
      Aderson's Department Store
      1917 Houston Avenue
      Pennsauken, N.J. 08110

      Dear Ms. Hamilton:

      Your recent job listing (10 February) was forwarded to me
      by Edward Jones, one of your salespeople. I note with
      special interest that you are seeking summer office help,
      and I would like very much to have you consider me for one
      of the positions.

      I am now completing my first year of business school at the
      University of Pennsylvania, where I plan to major in
      marketing. The past two summers I have been a retail clerk
      at Gray's Drug Company, but I now wish to broaden my
      business experiences. My college courses this year have
      provided me, I believe, a good base for the kind of general
      office work described in your listing.

      For further information regarding my qualifications,
      please contact Mr. H. W. Gray at (609) 663-4611. Also,
      Mrs. J. B. Markley, Principal of Pennsauken High School,
      and the Rev. Mr. David Muir, pastor of the First Methodist
      Church, have agreed to serve as character references for
      me.

      Since our spring semester here ends earlier than many
      other colleges, I would be available to begin work anytime
      after 6 May. If you wish to talk with me in person, I
      would be happy to come to your office at your convenience.
      My telephone number is (215) 543-4426.


      Sincerely yours,

      Robert John Thomas
      Robert John Thomas
```

615 CLAIM The letter of complaint or claim should always be courteous, digni-
fied, and fair. It should state exactly the cause for complaint and should outline clearly the reasonable adjustment expected. The complainants who
impute blame or become sarcastic or abusive only emphasize their own lack
of refinement and make less probable the adjustment sought. If the impression is given that it is taken for granted that one is dealing with those who are
absolutely honest and eager to make any reasonable adjustment, the complainant will seldom fail to get satisfaction. If one has had previous satisfactory dealings with the company, it is well to mention it to substantiate the
expressed confidence. Most companies are quick to respond favorably to a
justified complaint. The words *claim* or *complaint* are never used in such a
letter.

3636 Weldon Street
Dallas, Texas 75201
May 6, 19__

The Glacier Book Company
340 Vine Street
Denver, Colorado 80202

Gentlemen:

   On May the first I ordered from you one copy of
Magic Mountain by Dale Warwick. The book arrived by
mail today, and I found that some of the pages were
transposed so that the book was not usable. I should
like the privilege of returning the defective copy
of the book to you in exchange·for a perfect copy.

   I shall wait for instructions from you.

   You may be sure that I will appreciate your
adjusting the matter for me.

                          Yours sincerely,

                          H. C. Bradford
                          H. C. Bradford

616 ADJUSTMENT The writing of the letter of adjustment sometimes calls for
much diplomacy. Those who write letters of complaint often do so while
they are angry or in a disagreeable mood, but those who answer them should
do so in such a way as to promote good feeling. Even when the complainant
is very unreasonable and abusive, a reply showing courtesy and fairness is
usually most effective. When the requested adjustment is to be made, the
letter may be quite simple. An apologetic tone should be avoided, either
expressed or implied.

GLACIER
BOOK CO. 340 Vine Street   Denver, Colorado   80202

9 May 19__

Mr. H. C. Bradford
3636 Weldon Street
Dallas, Texas 75201

Dear Mr. Bradford:

     Thank you for calling our attention to the
imperfect copy of Magic Mountain. We regret that you
have been caused inconvenience, and we assure you that
we are glad to adjust the matter. We are sending you
by parcel post another copy of the work. We are
enclosing with this letter postage for the return of
the imperfect volume.

     We appreciate this opportunity of making our
service satisfactory and hope to continue to be of
service to you in the future.

                              Cordially yours,

                              L. W. Glade

LWG:EBK   L. W. Glade
Encl.   President

Exercise 8.1   Business Letters.

   a. Write a letter of application for a position that you feel you could competently fill. Prepare it completely (that is, type it neatly, fold it properly, and place it in an addressed envelope).

   b. Prepare typed business letters for two of the following:

1. Request the permission of a former teacher or employer to use his or her name as a reference.
2. Order four tickets to a concert to be held in a major city.
3. Request the circulation manager of a magazine to change your address and to renew your subscription.
4. Submit a claim to a recording company that is billing you for three tape cassettes that you ordered but have never received.

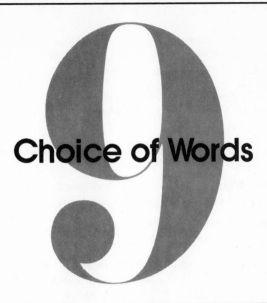

Choice of Words

A living language is constantly changing. Its standards of correctness are established by those who are considered its most authoritative users. Inexperienced writers and speakers especially should stay within the limits of those standards and use only words which are sanctioned by best authority. However, this standard of correctness may vary with the form of expression in which it is found. The formal literary type of expression would be out of place in a more informal situation requiring a colloquial type of expression. The report of a football game kept to the standard required for a formal essay would no doubt be rather dull reading. Even the standard required for the less formal kinds of writing might be altogether out of place in conversation.

Good English is that which is appropriate to the type of expression in which it is used. **Diction** as used here refers to the choice of words for accuracy, clarity, variety, and effectiveness rather than to its second meaning, the manner of the speaking, that is, the pronunciation and enunciation of public speakers and singers.

VARIETIES OF DICTION

617   There are types of expressions which are avoided by the best writers and speakers. But there are other types of word usage that are perfectly acceptable when appropriate to the situation. An understanding of this appropriateness marks the educated person. Most types of word usage may be classified

under the following headings: **archaic expressions, barbarisms, colloquialisms, improprieties, neologisms** (newly coined words), **provincialisms, slang, vulgarisms, hackneyed** or **trite expressions,** and **idiomatic expressions.**

618   ARCHAIC EXPRESSIONS   Words are archaic which have become old-fashioned and no longer are used naturally: *spirituous* (for *spirited*), *eftsoons* (for *soon after*), *methinks, avaunt.*

    ARCHAIC: The youthful crowd will be *convocated* here *anon.*
    MODERN: The young people will gather here soon.

619   BARBARISMS   Word distortions, such as *alright, complected, disremember, irregardless* are to be avoided in contemporary usage.

    BARBARISM: I *disremember* the incident.
    STANDARD: I do not remember the incident.

620   COLLOQUIALISMS   Some expressions are correctly used in informal conversation or in informal writing that are not appropriate in formal composition. The ordinary contractions, such as *doesn't, hasn't,* and *can't,* are examples of colloquialisms. The modern colloquial style of writing requires great skill except when it reflects reported speech.

    COLLOQUIAL: *It's funny* that he *doesn't* return.
    FORMAL: It is strange that he does not return.

621   IMPROPRIETIES   Good words may be used inappropriately, such as *set* for *sit, most* for *almost, accept* for *except, affect* for *effect:*

    IMPROPRIETY: It seems that *most all* the students are here.
    CORRECT: It seems that almost all the students are here.

622   NEOLOGISMS   Large numbers of words are added to the language or changed in meaning each year, and they are not necessarily to be avoided. When in doubt, check with an up-to-date dictionary.

    RECENTLY COINED: Have you heard about the *recycling* of waste materials? Computer *software* is now easily available.
    They go only to the most *trendy* shops.

623   PROVINCIALISMS   Dialectal words, often nonstandard and used by local people, are expressions peculiar to a region (province), such as *carry* (for accompany), *poke* (for bag or sack), *cayuse* (for range horse), *jolt wagon* (for farm wagon).

    PROVINCIAL: She cooked a meal in the *spider.*
    GENERAL: She cooked a meal in the frying pan.

624   SLANG   Are you a "square"? Or is square (to describe a person) so outdated that you would call anyone who used it a "turkey"? Both are terms of scorn; *square* is given in some dictionaries as a slang term to refer to a person who does not fit in with the "in" group; Turkey has reached the dictionary as

slang but may already have disappeared from common usage. Most slang is overworked and quickly worn to threads.

Slang may be the language of your group, but usually it would be wise not to use it in writing or in talking with older people. Adults may have at one time in their lives used a great deal of slang, but they know how tiresome and meaningless it may become. Still, slang is clever, forceful, or picturesque and may sometimes become part of the language of mature people—such words as *sob story, mob,* or *stooge* are now accepted. Slang should not be entirely despised, but it should be used with care.

Various terms are associated with slang in describing non-standard usage: **dialect, patois, argot, jargon, cant, vernacular.** Each has its own particular application. See your dictionary.

625 **VULGARISMS** Some words are never correct in either formal or informal expression: words such as *blowed, brung, busted* (for burst), *drawed, drownded, et, growed, hain't, hern, hisn, hisself, knowed, nowheres, scairt, theirn, theirselves, them there,* and *this here.* The term also applies to obscenities.

626 **HACKNEYED OR TRITE EXPRESSIONS** Phrases that have been over-used until they have almost lost their effectiveness are **trite.** Although young writers are tempted to use these worn-out expressions or clichés, they should learn to substitute more vital ones. Some of the hackneyed terms frequently used are *brave as a lion, brown as a berry, busy as a bee, cold as ice, green as grass, pearls before swine.*

627 **IDIOMATIC EXPRESSIONS** Idioms are expressions that are peculiar to every language and often they are not governed by the rules of its grammar; therefore it is difficult to translate them into another language. Idioms, though they may defy analysis within the rules of grammar, have nevertheless become through long-continued usage firmly established as standard.

That these expressions at first glance may not be parsed or diagrammed should not discourage their use. The very best writers of all languages make constant use of idioms. Some common English idioms are *put up with, all of a sudden, get rid of it, in the long run, get into hot water, with a grain of salt.* Be careful to use correct idioms. The prepositions especially are often determined by their idiomatic use rather than by logic:

UNIDIOMATIC: Hal was accompanied *with* his brother.
CORRECT: Hal was accompanied *by* his brother. (See 355.)

USAGE GLOSSARY

628 Some of the expressions listed here are in established use in **informal speech and writing,** but standard usage calls for the more **formal expression in writing.** Remember, however, that usage changes. Learn to check with the dictionary.

Accept—except. *Accept* means *to take* or *receive*. *Except* (verb) means *to exclude* or *leave out*. As a preposition it means *but* or *excluding*.

I *accept* a gift.
We voted to *except* these members from service.
All the gifts *except* yours were returned.

Affect—effect. *Affect* is a transitive verb meaning *to influence* or *to pretend*. *Effect* as a verb means *to bring about; effect* as a noun means *result:*

The noise *affects* (not *effects*) my hearing.
They *effected* (not *affected*) a compromise.
His work had a good *effect* (not *affect*).

All ready—already. *All ready* means everything or everyone is ready. *Already* is an adverb meaning "by this time."

The guests had come *already*.
We were *all ready* for the fun.

All right. Use the phrase *all right* rather than *alright*; the latter word is recorded but, as yet, with little approval for use.

Is it *all right* (not *alright*) to take the car?

All together—altogether. *All together* means "in a group." *Altogether* is an adverb meaning "completely."

This is *altogether* bad.
They were *all together* in the boat.

Allusion—illusion. An *allusion* is an indirect or implied reference (from the verb "to allude"). If a sportswriter refers to a long-haired athlete as one who is "afraid that a barber might steal his strength," he is making an allusion to the biblical Samson. An *illusion*, however, is completely different in meaning: a false impression or deception. "A photograph can sometimes give one the illusion that a person's feet are enormous."

A lot. Always two words (not *alot*).

Alternative. This word means a *choice between two things*.

He had the *alternative* of resigning or of being fired.

Among—between. It is still considered good usage to distinguish between these two prepositions. When more than two people or things are concerned, use *among* ("among the team members"). Reserve the use of *between* for dealing only with two people or things ("between you and me").

Anybody. An indefinite pronoun written as one word.

Any more. Written as two words.

Anyone. An indefinite pronoun written as one word. *Any one* (written as two words) mean "any single person or thing": "There are three buses leaving at noon: you may take any one."

At. Do not use *at* unnecessarily with *where*:

Where is the book *at*? (Omit *at*.)

Awful. This term originally meant *awe-inspiring*, but it has been so weakened by its colloquial use that it can seldom be used in its original meaning. *Awful* and *awfully* should be avoided in most writing since they are merely general terms of emphasis or disapproval:

Jane is *unusually* (not *awfully*) smart.
This was a *difficult* (not an *awful*) job.

Badly. In formal writing do not use this adverb in the sense of *very much* nor as a predicate adjective (289)

I want *very much* (not *badly*) to succeed.
He looks *bad* (not *badly*) since his illness.

Complected. This is a barbarism.

She is *light-complexioned* (not *light-complected*).

Considerable. Use this term as an adjective; rarely as a noun.

A *considerable* sum of money is invested in that plant.
They have done *considerable* for the school. **(informal)**

Credible–credulous. Credible means *believable;* credulous means *believing too easily:*

That is a *credible* story.
He was too *credulous* in accepting their account.

Criteria. The plural of *criterion.* It is never correct to say *a* criteria.

Data. The plural of *datum. Data* should not be used in reference to a single piece of information. Use *fact* or *figure* instead.

Different from. Usually preferable to *different than.*

Due to. Although some authorities object to this phrase, it is generally accepted in daily usage. Because it almost always sounds stuffy, however, it is usually wiser to replace it with *because of, though,* or *since.*

Either–neither. Best used to indicate one of two persons or things:

None (not *neither*) of the four boys would go.
Either of the *two* girls can take the part.

Everybody–everyone. Both of these are usually regarded as singular and thus take singular verbs and pronoun references:

Everybody thinks *his* idea is worthy of consideration.

Expect   In formal writing do not confuse *expect*, meaning *to anticipate*, with *suppose*, meaning *to be of the opinion*:

I *suppose* (not *expect*) he is wealthy.
We *expect* to see you tomorrow.

Farther–further.   The distinction between *farther* to refer to *spatial distance* and *further* to refer to *time, degree,* or *quantity* is waning but it is still observed by many careful writers:

We walked *farther* than two miles.
I shall go no *further* with this business.
The explorer went *further* into the forest.

Fix.   This is colloquial when used to mean *predicament, difficult situation,* or *condition* and badly overused:

I was in a desperate *situation* (not *fix*) about my grades.

Formally–formerly.   *Formally* means *in a formal manner; formerly* means *previously:*

The guest was treated *formally*.
He was *formerly* mayor of the town.

Funny.   Do not use for *odd* or *strange*, except in colloquial expressions:

It is *strange* (not *funny*) that he lost his fortune.

Gentleman–lady.   These terms are sometimes applied to show respect but are more often merely pretentious. Of course, in addressing an audience the speaker still may correctly say: "Ladies and gentlemen." The terms *man* and *woman* are best for general use:

I met a pleasant woman (not *lady*) at the museum.

Get up.   This two-word verb in the meaning of *organize, prepare,* or *arrange,* is now acceptable for general use, though it is informal in feeling.

They *got up* a good party for the team.

Good.   Do not use the adjective *good* as an adverb (329):

He sings *well* (not *good*).

Got.   *Got*, with *had, has,* or *have* to indicate possession or obligation emphatically, is generally acceptable in informal usage.

He *has got* the money here.
I *have got* to go immediately.

Had ought to.   Do not use *had ought to* for *ought to* or *should:*

You *ought* (not *had ought*) to write to Ned.
You *should* (not *had ought to*) read this book.

Imply–infer.   A speaker or writer may *imply* more than he says, the hearer *infers* what the speaker intends:

We *inferred* from what Jim said that he was angry with us.
The speaker did not *imply* that anyone in particular was to blame.

In back of.   Wordy for *behind.*

Irregardless.   Unacceptable. Simply use *regardless.*

Its—it's.   *Its* is the possessive pronoun. *It's* is the contraction of *it is.*

The group had lost *its* enthusiasm.
It's time to go home.

Kind of—sort of.   It is still much better not to use these terms for *rather* or *somewhat* (333).

He seems *rather* (not *sort of* or *kind of*) tired.

Lay—lie.   *Lay* is usually transitive and takes a receiver of its action; its principal parts are *lay—laid—laid.* *Lie* is intransitive in its usual meanings and does not take an object; its principal parts are *lie—lay—lain* (but see 217).

Did you *lay* (not *lie*) the rake on the ground?
You should not *lie* (not *lay*) on the wet grass.

Learn—teach.   To *learn* means to *get knowledge;* to *teach* means to *give knowledge* (227).

You should *learn* to play tennis.
Teach me how to swim.

Less—fewer.   *Less* refers to *quantity; fewer* refers to *number:*

This lake has *less* water than the other.
This tree has *fewer* branches than that.

Liable—likely.   *Likely* means *probably; liable* means *responsible for* or it may refer to a *possibility with unpleasant results:*

He is *likely* (not *liable*) to win the race.
He is *liable* for his own debts.
He is *liable* to harm someone.

Like.   In formal writing do not use *like* for *as, as if,* or *as though,* in introducing a clause:

Do *as* (not *like*) I do.
He acted *as if* (not *like*) he knew it and *as though* (not *like*) he had always known it.

Mad.   Do not use *mad* for *angry* in formal situations, though both are standard, for *mad* implies "insane" to many people.

John was *angry* (not *mad*) because of the delay.

Most.   Do not use the adjective *most* for the adverb *almost* (328); note also that *almost* modifies indefinite pronouns: *almost* everybody, *almost* anyone (316):

We sold *almost* (not *most*) all the tickets.

None. This word has long been accepted as singular or plural:

None *were* pleased with the result.
None of the girls *was* present.

Of—have. The use of the preposition *of* in place of the verb *have* is nonstandard:

I should *have* (not should *of*) remembered.

Off—from. Do not misuse *off* or *off of* for *from:*

He bought the book *from* (not *off* or *off of*) me.

Off of. The *of* is superfluous; when used it is informal.

He jumped *off* (not *off of*) the car.

Party. Do not use for *person* except in terms of law or in a jocular sense.

I saw the *person* (not *party*) who won the prize.

Principal—principle. *Principal* is a noun meaning "chief official" or an adjective meaning "chief" or "main." *Principle* is a noun meaning "fundamental truth."

Quotation—quote. *Quotation* is a noun; *quote* is a verb.

The following quotation is from *Hamlet.*
Professor Bowden liked to quote from Shakespeare.

Raise—rear. Raise is now in good standard usage for "bring up" without distinction of kind, but the following distinctions have been made up to now.

They *reared* three children.
He *raised* hogs for market.

Raise—rise. In its usual meanings *raise* is transitive and takes a receiver of its action; its principal parts are *raise—raised—raised. Rise* is intransitive and almost never takes an object; its principal parts are *rise—rose—risen* (217): Neither needs to be followed by *up:*

Jim *raised* (not *rose*) the window.
The plane *rose* (not *raised*) quickly as it flew away.

Real. Avoid using the adjective *real* for the adverbs *very* or *really* (311).

She is *very* (not *real*) talented and *really* well educated.
His boat was in *real* (actual) danger.

Reason. A statement containing *the reason is* is preferably completed by a *that* clause:

The reason he succeeded is *that* (not *because*) he worked hard.

Set–sit. *Set* is usually transitive and takes a receiver of its action; its principal parts are *set–set–set*. *Sit* is usually intransitive and does not take an object; its principal parts are *sit–sat–sat* (217):

Set (not *sit*) the chair in the corner.
We *sat* (not *set*) on the grass to rest.

So. Do not use it as an intensive in formal writing:

He is *extremely* (not *so*) careful.

That–which–who. Generally it is best to use *that* in restrictive clauses modifying objects or animals: "The car that stalls is now being repaired." Use *which* in nonrestrictive (nonessential or parenthetical) clauses modifying things or animals: "Our car, which occasionally stalls, is now being repaired." Use *who* for people in either restrictive or nonrestrictive clauses: "The women, who were all teachers, met every Friday."

Thusly. Unacceptable. Simply use *thus*.

Try and. Avoid this construction, replacing it with *try to*.

Unique. This word, by definition, means "one of a kind." Something cannot be "rather unique" or "really unique" or "somewhat unique." It's unique, or it is not.

Wait on. Do not use the dialectal *wait on* for *wait for:*

Do not *wait for* (not *wait on*) me if my plane is late.

Way–ways. Use the singular form in sentences like this:

He rode a short *way* (not *ways*) with us.

Who's–whose. *Who's* is the contraction of *who is*. *Whose* is the possessive pronoun.

Who's going to the game?
Whose hat is this?

You're–your. *You're* is the contraction for *you are*. *Your* is the possessive pronoun.

You're mistaken. *Your* paper is not on my desk.

PRONUNCIATION

629 The only sure guide to correct pronunciation is a good standard dictionary. Be careful, however, to read the entries thoroughly. Some words (called *heteronyms*, see 638) are identical in spelling but differ significantly in pronunciation, meaning, and origin. For instance, a *bass* is a species of fish, but a different *bass* is a musical term for both a male vocal part and a musical instrument. Other words, such as *economy* (noun) and *economic* (adjective),

or *envelop* (verb) and *envelope* (noun), are close in appearance but considerably different in pronunciation. Yet other words have but one meaning while having two or three acceptable pronunciations, one of which is preferred over the others. It takes only a short time to check the correct pronunciation in a dictionary, but it is often necessary if you wish to avoid embarrassment.

FIGURES OF SPEECH

630   A **figure of speech** is a variation from the ordinary method of expression for the sake of effect. Though there are many figures of speech, the two in most common use are the **simile** and the **metaphor**. Others are **personification, hyperbole, metonymy,** and **synecdoche**. Figures of speech are employed effectively in both prose and poetry.

631   A **simile** is a direct comparison, introduced by *like* or *as,* of two things which in their general nature are different from each other:

She is *like* a shining star.   His hair is black *as* night.

632   A **metaphor** is implied comparison. Instead of stating the comparison, as in the simile, the likeness is suggested by terms not literally applicable to each other:

She is a *shining star.*   A *wave of emotion* overcame him.

633   Do not use mixed metaphors, such as these:

He is *aflame* with a *thirst* for knowledge.
Life is not all a rough *sea;* sometimes its *pathway* is smooth.

When a **simile** or a **metaphor** becomes involved and farfetched, it is called a **conceit**.

634   **Personification** is the figure of speech in which some human characteristic is attributed to an inanimate thing:

The *friendly* hills seemed to *welcome* us.

635   **Hyperbole** is exaggeration for the purpose of emphasis and without any intention of being taken literally:

I am *completely starved.*

636   **Metonymy** is the substitution of the name of the whole for the name of the part, while **synecdoche** is the substitution of the part for the whole.

I am reading *Stevenson* (i.e., a book or poem by him).
This *camera* is broken (i.e., some part of it is broken).
They were stopped by a *badge* (i.e., a man with a badge, a policeman).
The ships dipped their *colors* (i.e., their flags).

SYLLABICATION

637 Syllabication was originally a device of early printers to break words at the end of the printed line in order to give equal spacing between words and to keep the right margin aligned and parallel with the left margin. In general, the division in printed form follows the syllables of the spoken language. But, as there are so many exceptions due to the variations in the spelling and derivation of English words, the only sure guide to ascertain the current use is to refer to a good dictionary rather than to rely on one's ear.

EXAMPLE: syl-lab-i-ca-tion (spelled). si-lab-i-ca-tion (pronounced). The following rules should be followed in handwriting and typing:

a. Never divide words pronounced as one syllable: *drowned*.
b. Never divide words of two syllables with one a single vowel: *even, over*.
c. Do not divide the parts of a name: *John Smith, Mr. Jones*.
d. Do not divide numbers or abbreviations: *10,000, C.O.D., SOS*.
e. Do not divide endings such as: *-tial, -tion, -cious, -geous*.
f. Do not separate a final syllable of one or two letters: *-a, -ed, -es*.
g. Do not divide hyphened compounds except at the hyphen.

Spelling—Words Often Confused

638 English, like other languages, has a number of paired words that cause confusion. There are four classes of such words.

1. Heteronyms. These words are identical in spelling, but they differ in origin, pronunciation, and meaning:

bass, fish; *bass*, male voice, musical term
row, a line; *row*, a fight

2. Homographs. These words are identical in spelling, but they differ in origin, meaning, and sometimes in pronunciation:

fair, market; *fair*, beautiful
wind, air current; *wind*, to coil

3. Homonyms. These words are identical in spelling and pronunciation, but they differ in origin and meaning:

butter, food; *butter*, one who butts
pool, water; *pool*, the game

4. Homophones. These words are identical in pronunciation, but they differ in origin, spelling, and meaning:

fair, market; *fare*, food and drink; *fare*, tariff
red, color; *read*, past tense of *read*

639   Here are **homophones** which everyone should be able to spell and define correctly (in English there are at least three hundred seventy-five such paired word groups):

aisle–isle	die–dye	made–maid
all–awl	done–dun	mail–male
altar–alter	earn–urn	main–mane
ant–aunt	fain–feign	manner–manor
arc–ark	faint–feint	mantel–mantle
ascent–assent	fair–fare	meat–meet
ate–eight	feat–feet	medal–meddle
aught–ought	fir–fur	might–mite
bail–bale	flea–flee	miner–minor
bait–bate	flew–flue	moan–mown
ball–bawl	flour–flower	muscle–mussel
bare–bear	fore–four	night–knight
base–bass	foul–fowl	none–nun
be–bee	freeze–frieze	one–won
beach–beech	gait–gate	pail–pale
beat–beet	great–grate	pain–pane
beau–bow	groan–grown	pause–paws
been–bin	guest–guessed	pair–pare–pear
bell–belle	hair–hare	peace–piece
berth–birth	hale–hail	peal–peel
bier–beer	hall–haul	plain–plane
blew–blue	hart–heart	pore–pour
board–bored	heal–heel	pray–prey
born–borne	hear–here	pride–pried
bough–bow	heard–herd	principal–principle
brake–break	heir–air	profit–prophet
buy–by	hew–hue	rain–rein–reign
calendar–calender	hoes–hose	raise–raze
canvas–canvass	hole–whole	read–reed
capital–capitol	holy–wholly	read–red
ceiling–sealing	hour–our	real–reel
cell–sell	idol–idle	rest–wrest
cellar–seller	in–inn	rhyme–rime
cent–sent–scent	jam–jamb	right–write–wright–rite
cereal–serial	kernel–colonel	ring–wring
choir–quire	knead–need	road–rode–rowed
chord–cord	knew–new	role–roll
clause–claws	knot–not	rose–rows
coarse–course	know–no	rough–ruff
complement–compliment	lain–lane	rye–wry
council–counsel	lead–led	sail–sale
creak–creek	lessen–lesson	scene–seen
currant–current	lie–lye	sea–see
dear–deer	load–lode	seam–seem
dew–due	loan–lone	seine–sane

sew—sow—so	stationary—stationery	vice—vise
shone—shown	steal—steel	wade—weighed
sight—site—cite	stile—style	waist—waste
slay—sleigh	straight—strait	wait—weight
sleight—slight	suite—sweet	ware—wear
slew—slue—slough	tail—tale	warn—worn
soar—sore	their—there	wave—waive
sole—soul	threw—through	way—weigh
some—sum	throne—thrown	week—weak
son—sun	to—too—two	whole—hole
staid—stayed	toe—tow	whose—who's
stair—stare	vail—veil—vale	wood—would
stake—steak	vain—vane—vein	

SPELLING

640   THE WRITTEN WORD   An essential characteristic of good writing is correct spelling.   American English in its written form was initially recorded in Samuel Johnson's first American dictionary published in New Haven, Connecticut, in 1798.   This Samuel Johnson was not related to Doctor Samuel Johnson, the sage of Fleet Street, whose famous English dictionary was published in London in 1755.

In the American Johnson's work the beginnings of simplified spelling first appeared, later to be amplified in Noah Webster's *American Dictionary* of 1828:   There is for the English language no authoritative arbiter of usage such as the *Academie Francaise* or the *Accademia della Crusa* of France and Italy "to sift the husks and purify the language."   In general, dictionaries of the English language rely on recording the language as it is "used" rather than "how it ought to be."   It is inevitable then that different dictionaries will reflect the tastes of different times, different places, and different lexicographers.   Nevertheless, there is such a wide area of agreement in our standard American English spelling that a misspelled word is inexcusable.

Spelling List and Vocabulary Builder

641   The words in this list should be learned and mastered as they comprise a working vocabulary of high frequency and usefulness.   Most of these words are among those frequently misspelled by writers and printers alike.

♦ The homophones, in section 639, are not repeated in this list. They should be added to the list as a genuine part of a good vocabulary.   To illustrate, consider this EXAMPLE: An important spelling error may occur, when we permit the "advice" of *counsel* to "advise" us to speak out in the *council*, although we were ruled out of order by the council chairperson.

♦ The principal parts of irregular verbs, in section 204, are also to be considered as a part of this spelling list and should be learned for both their correct use and their spelling in writing. EXAMPLE: Now that I *know* him—and *knowing* him as well as I do—I *knew* that I should have *known* all about him before this.

abridgment	beginning	dependent
absence	believe	description
accelerate	beneficial	desirable
accessible	bourgeois	despair
accidentally	bourgeoisie	desperate
accommodate	Britain	develop
achievement	bureau	dilemma
acknowledgment	bureaucracy	disappear
acquire	burglar	disappoint
across	business	disastrous
actually	calendar	divide
address	cannot	divine
adjacent	candidate	ecstasy
adolescence	career	eighth
adolescent	category	embarrass
advice (noun)	cemetery	envelop (verb)
advise (verb)	changeable	envelope (noun)
aggravate	chief	environment
aggressive	choose (distinguish	equipped
aging	from past tense)	equivalent
alcohol	chosen	especially
allege	commit	essence
all right	committee	exaggerate
a lot	comparative	exceed
already	competent	excellence
altogether	congratulate	excellent
amateur	conscience	exhilarate
analysis	conscious	existence
analyze	consistent	experience
apologize	controversy	explanation
apparent	convenient	familiar
appreciate	coolly	fascinate
arctic	corollary	foreign
argument	correspondence	forty
assassin	counterfeit	fourth
assistance	criticism	freight
assistant	curiosity	friend
athlete	deceive	gauge
attendance	decision	genealogy
awkward	defendant	goddess
bargain	definite	government
beggar	deity	grammar

grateful
grievance
guarantee
height
heroes
hoping
hypocrisy
imagination
immediately
impel
incidentally
incredible
independence
independent
indispensable
insistence
insistent
intelligent
interest
interpretation
interrupt
irrelevant
irresistible
judgment
led (past tense
of "to lead")
leisure
license
livelihood
loneliness
lonely
loose (adjective)
lose (verb)
losing
maintenance
maneuver
marriage
mathematics
medicine
mileage
misspell
necessary
necessity
niece
ninety
noticeable
nuclear
occasion
occasionally

occur
occurred
occurrence
omit
omitted
original
parallel
pastime
peaceable
performance
permanent
persistent
personnel
playwright
possession
practically
precede
predominant
preferred
prejudice
prevalent
privilege
probability
probably
procedure
proceed
professor
prominent
prophecy (noun)
prophesy (verb)
psychiatry
psychology
pursue
quantity
questionnaire
realize
really
receipt
receive
recommend
referring
relevance
relevant
relieve
religious
remembrance
repentance
repetition
resistance

rhyme
rhythm
sacrifice
secretary
seize
sense
separate
shining
shriek
similar
solely
specimen
sponsor
strategy
strength
subtlety
subtly
succeed
supersede
surprise
syllable
technique
temperament
tendency
theories
thorough
tragedy
transferred
tried
truly
unanimous
unnecessary
useful
usually
various
vengeance
villain
weird
whether
withhold
writing
yield
zealous

642   THE DICTIONARY AS A TOOL   One of the areas of difference in usage is, of course, the spelling of the words and forms of the written language. The young writer will find that the best tool for controlling this aspect of expression is the dictionary. Its constant use is a *must*. The dictionary verifies one's spelling when there is doubt; where more than one form is acceptable, it records them in one place; when certain spellings have restricted application, it states the fact; and when regional differences affect the choice of form (American vs. British, standard vs. dialectal, serious vs. humorous, for example), the dictionary indicates the preference.

COMPOUNDING

643   English compound words give much spelling trouble to writers everywhere, because there are so many of them. Here is an area where the "rules" applicable are often at variance with actual usage. Memorize as many as you can. In fact, several books detailing the technique have been written about the compounding of English words. Note these few illustrative examples—of the large number of patterns possible:

airplane	= noun + noun
press agent	= noun (used as adjective) + noun
spoilsport	= verb + noun
good-looking	= adjective + participle
uptown	= adverb + noun
newlywed	= adverb + participle
newly wed couple	= adverb + participle + noun
old-age pension	= adjective + noun + noun
Mexican-American	= proper adjective + proper adjective

What is an English compound word? It is the combination of several standard words which, when used together, create a new concept of meaning. Thus, every *black bird* is not necessarily a *blackbird;* a *workingman* does not mean a *man* is *working;* a *storeroom* does not mean a *room* in a *store;* a *cornflower* is not the *flower* of the *corn* plant. Each compound, then, becomes a word in its own right.

There are three types of compounds to be considered and one of these (3) is not technically a compound: (1) The solid form—*outlaw, textbook,* (to) *shortchange* (solideme); (2) the hyphenated form—*X-Ray, city-state, well-known* (hypheme); (3) the word-phrase form of two or more words—*red tape, printing press, post office, one hundred and one* (men), *three week's* (pay). Your dictionary is the proper source for determining what is the actual and correct form to be used in writing. Once you have chosen the correct form, always be consistent in using it.

644   THE UNIT MODIFIER   This hyphened form is a conventional, recorded two-noun phrase or an improvised literal compound adjective which is used only before a noun:

cast iron   — a *cast-iron* bridge
gas meter   — a *gas-meter* reading
folk dance   — a *folk-dance* festival
rush hour   — a *rush-hour* crush
air mail   — an *air-mail* letter
             — an *ever-winding* road
             — an *always-smoking* chimney
             — a *reddish-brown* paint
             — an *off-and-on* game
             — a *tongue-in-cheek* remark

ABOUT WORDS

645   FOREIGN WORDS AND PHRASES   This class of words must be carefully checked as to spelling, including accent marks, and as to whether they are or are not considered anglicized: that is, whether or not they should be italicized as foreign words or phrases:

auf Wiedersehn   — German
au fait   — French
amuck   — Malayan: *amock*
Calvary   — Late Latin: *Calvaria*
Cordoba   — Spanish: *Cordova*
Van Gogh [van go] — Dutch: *van Khokh*
habeas corpus   — English Law Latin (1679)

646   VOCABULARY   The ability to express one's thoughts and to understand the expression of the thoughts of others can be measured by one's knowledge of the meaning of words. A good and expressive vocabulary is, obviously, an invaluable aid to success in any field. It must include the words in the vocabularies of the student's special fields of interest—be it art, music, engineering, agriculture, space science, or ecology—with their **synonyms** (words of the same general meaning but different in their specific application) and **antonyms** (words of opposite meaning).

647   THE USE OF THE DICTIONARY   The use of a standard unabridged dictionary is valuable in building a vocabulary. It gives extensive information about every word—pronunciation, part of speech, derivation, illustrations of current usage, various meanings, synonyms, and antonyms. In a section, usually at the front of the dictionary, all the symbols used in its pronunciation system are explained, and the diacritical marks are fully illustrated.

648   A PLAN FOR VOCABULARY BUILDING   To develop a good, working vocabulary requires time, patience, and persistence. One good plan is to write in a notebook all unfamiliar words that one reads or hears. Unfamiliar words and word uses found in reading one's own books should be marked so that the meaning may be studied in context (650). A periodic review of what has been noted reinforces learning.

649   SPECIAL-SUBJECT DICTIONARIES AND GLOSSARIES   Almost every area of knowledge today has its own special vocabulary of words and terms. Sometimes they are included as a part of a book on a given subject to show how the author has used them in developing the subject. At times the use may differ, in some limiting aspect, from the standard definition of a word or phrase. A compilation of such word-usage is called a **glossary**. It may be included within a book as an appendix, or it may be extensive enough to be issued as a separate book or pamphlet.

In vocabulary building, such dictionaries and glossaries should not be overlooked, for they are a rich source of specialized information.

650   WORDS IN CONTEXT   Context may be simply defined as the "weaving together of words." More formally it is described as "any phrase, sentence, or passage so closely connected to a word or words as to affect their meaning."

Thus the association of words with each other is important in vocabulary building. To illustrate, consider the word *eye,* the organ of vision in animals. By various figures of speech we have: a *black* eye (area); *brown* eye (color of the iris of the eye); keep an *eye* on (watch carefully); cast an *eye* over (look at); in the public *eye* (in the presence of); an evil *eye* (particular expression of); an *eye* for girls (interest in); the *eye* of the riot (focal point); the *eye* of the storm (central area); electric *eye* (in resemblance to the human eye); *eye* of the wind (direction); *eye* to *eye* (in agreement with).

Index

Numbers refer to the sections of this book.